No-Work

PAPERWORK
for Children's Ministry

Group
Loveland, Colorado

No-Work Paperwork for Children's Ministry

Credits

Contributing Authors: Melissa Downey, Nanette Goings, Lori Haynes Niles, Liz Shockey, and Kim West
Book Acquisition Editor: Susan L. Lingo
Editor: Jan Kershner
Creative Products Director: Joani Schultz
Copy Editor: Sandra Collier
Art Director and Designer: Lisa Chandler
Computer Graphic Artist: Kari K. Monson
Cover Art Director: Liz Howe
Cover Designer: Bill Fisher
Cover Illustrator: DeWain Stoll
Illustrators: Jan Knudson and Kari K. Monson
Production Manager: Ann Marie Gordon

Unless otherwise noted, Scriptures quoted from The Youth Bible, New Century Version, copyright © 1991 by Word Publishing, Dallas, Texas 75039. Used by permission.

Library of Congress Cataloging-in-Publication Data
No-work paperwork for children's ministry.
    p.   cm.
   ISBN 1-55945-621-3 (alk. paper)
   1. Church work with children–Forms. 2. Sunday schools–Forms.
I. Group Publishing.
BV639.C4N6 1996
259' .22'068–dc20

95-50582
CIP

ISBN 1-55945-621-3
10 9 8 7 6 5 4 3 2 1   05 04 03 02 01 00 99 98 97 96
Printed in the United States of America.

Contents

Introduction

Children are energetic, open, spontaneous, and fun. And that's how you'd like your children's ministry to be, too. Right?

But with all the planning, record-keeping, volunteer recruitment, and funding concerns, it isn't easy.

Don't let your ministry become mired in administrative mayhem. Let the forms in *No-Work Paperwork for Children's Ministry* help you make the most of your time and talents. In the following chapters you'll find

- calendars and checklists to make every event run smoothly
- expense logs to keep costs under control
- evaluation forms to keep you in tune with your group
- permission and release forms to limit liability
- request forms and thank you notes to keep helpers happy
- invitations and affirmations to keep kids coming back
- surveys and shopping lists to save time
- VBS guidelines to keep your summer program sailing smoothly

Every form you'll ever need for successful children's ministry is included in *No-Work Paperwork*. Get the most from these forms by using the Terrific Tips that accompany them. You may even want to color code your files and the paper you use when you photocopy specific forms: blue for meetings, white for checklists, yellow for reminders, and green for agendas.

We're sure the forms in *No-Work Paperwork* will help you become, and stay, more organized than you ever thought possible. And with less of your time going to paperwork, you'll have more time to devote to the children God has entrusted to you!

1

Instant Organization!

Ever wonder how some people make organization look so effortless? The forms in this chapter are designed to make YOU one of those people!

- Conduct concise and fruitful meetings.
- Plan and publicize events with greater productivity.
- Be ready to staff when the need arises.
- Know "where to go" for answers to church and community questions.

With these forms at your fingertips, you'll be able to share important information and delegate responsibility with ease.

Super Shopper

When you're shopping for everyday supplies, nothing enhances organization as much as a checklist. Don't return from the store with a big box of markers only to find that there are three boxes tucked in the back of a closet. Never run out of graham crackers or glue...or any other little essentials that keep your kids humming! The Super Shopper checklist form can double as your shopping list—saving you precious time and money.

Terrific Tips

Super Shopper

✔ Make a complete inventory of supplies before implementing this checklist to avoid duplicate purchases. Then use the cost column to keep a running tally while at the store.

✔ Post a photocopy of this checklist on your supply room door so teachers can mark the items as needed. (Attach a pencil on a string for convenience.)

✔ Place a large "Coupons—Donations Welcome" envelope near your list. Match items on the list to coupons, then take both to the store for instant savings—in time and dollars!

✔ Since it's broken down by department, your checklist will work as well in a superstore or membership warehouse as it does in a neighborhood supermarket.

Super Shopper

Office Supplies

QTY.	ITEM	COST
_____	Pencils and pens_____	_____
_____	Copier paper (color?) _____	_____
_____	Paper clips (size?) _____	_____
_____	Masking or transparent tape	_____
_____	Correction tape or fluid	_____
_____	Computer disks	_____
_____	Computer paper	_____
_____	Envelopes (size) _____	_____
_____	Stamps	_____
_____	Other _____	_____
_____	_____	

Classroom

QTY.	ITEM	COST
_____	Construction paper (colors)_____	_____
_____	Glue or glue sticks	_____
_____	Markers and crayons	_____
_____	Poster board	_____
_____	Paints (type and colors) _____	_____
_____	Yarn or string (color) _____	_____
_____	Diapers	_____
_____	Baby wipes	_____
_____	Special stuff_____	_____
_____	_____	

Groceries

QTY.	ITEM	COST
_____	Crackers (type) _____	_____
_____	Juice	_____
_____	Fruit	_____
_____	Napkins	_____
_____	Paper plates	_____
_____	Cups	_____
_____	Utensils	_____
_____	Special treats _____	_____
_____	_____	

Maintenance

QTY.	ITEM	COST
_____	Rubber gloves	_____
_____	Soap	_____
_____	Paper towels	_____
_____	Disinfectant spray	_____
_____	Other _____	_____

The Big Event

Make the countdown to a big event easy with this convenient planning checklist. Not only will you stay on task, but you can keep your co-workers informed of changes and progress. Volunteers will appreciate the overview, and you will have delegated yourself into smooth sailing!

Terrific Tips

The Big Event

✔ Fill in the pertinent facts and give a photocopy of this form to your committee chairpersons, along with a Super Shopper form found on p. 7. (Designate a date the shopping lists need to be turned in to you.)

✔ In the committee boxes, jot down notes about your follow-up communication with each committee chairperson.

✔ Use this form to keep track of your progress, then file it to use as a basis for future planning.

THE BiG EVENT

TITLE:

DATE:

TIME:

PURPOSE:

OVERALL BUDGET:

GEARING UP

Six Months Before:

_____
_____
_____

Three Months Before:

_____
_____
_____

One Month Before:

_____
_____
_____

Final Week:

_____
_____
_____

Day Before:

_____
_____
_____

The Big Day:

_____
_____
_____

THE EVENT

DECORATIONS CHAIR _____
Phone #

Budget

ACTIVITIES CHAIR_____
Phone #

Budget

FOOD CHAIR _____
Phone #

Budget

PUBLICITY CHAIR _____
Phone #

Budget

CHAIR_____
Phone #

Budget

CHAIR _____
Phone #

Budget

GEARING DOWN

_____ Clean up planned

_____ Evaluations

_____ Worker appreciation

_____ Notes and workers for next year

Dynamite Meetings

A well-planned meeting can stop the fidgets before they begin! Use these handy notes to make sure everything you need is within arm's reach, then turn your full attention to the kids you love to teach!

Terrific Tips

Dynamite Meetings

✔ Keep a photocopy of this form handy as you prepare for your lesson. Jot down notes that come to mind and attach the form to the first page of your lesson.

✔ Place the materials for each activity in separate large envelopes. Label each one, then stack them in the order they are to be used in the lesson. That way you can simply grab each activity's envelope when you're ready, instead of wasting time trying to locate supplies.

✔ Use the "Who's Missing" section to follow up on kids who missed your time together.

dYNaMite Meetings

Supplies Needed:

Before the Meeting:

Equipment:

Don't Forget:

Books:

Who's Missing:

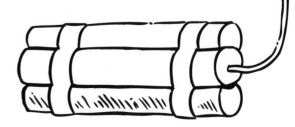

A Bird's Eye View

Meetings can be the most (or least) productive times in your week. Make every minute count by planning the details of your next meeting. Give your participants a preview of what needs to be accomplished during your time together. Then keep track of all the decisions you've made and the suggestions you've gathered to assure quick and painless follow-through!

Terrific Tips

A Bird's Eye View

✔ State your topics briefly and put a name next to any topics to be introduced by someone other than yourself.

✔ Keep on task by planning a time frame for each topic.

✔ Distribute the agenda several days before the meeting so that those involved will have a chance to think through their ideas.

✔ Take notes during the meeting to ensure accurate action.

A Bird's Eye View

Meeting of: _____ Date: _____

Time: _____ to _____

Location: _____

Publicity: _____ Calls made: _____ Reminders sent: _____

Who's Invited?

_____

_____

TOPIC:	SUGGESTIONS:	DECISIONS/ASSIGNMENTS:
1.		
2.		
3.		
4.		
5.		

If you have anything to add to this agenda, contact _____ by _____.

Pass It On!

You know the saying…"The shortest distance between two points is a straight line." Use these handy cover sheets to keep your communications on track. You'll easily share important material, since your item's route is determined in advance. (You'll also know where to look in case of a "kink in the line.")

Terrific Tips

Pass It On!

✔ Use a stamp with your name, address, and phone number to identify your originals.

✔ Attach your routing slips with removable tape—any kind of paper then functions like a self-stick note, which can be reattached without damaging a surface.

✔ If you're routing several pages, put them in a file folder or envelope and attach the routing slip to the outside.

✔ Keep a copy of the routing slip to remind yourself who needed to see the information.

Race This to the Finish Line!

Date _____ Please read and initial the attached information as soon as you can, then pass it to the next checkered flag! Please return to _____ by _____.

Pastor

Associate Pastor(s)

Music Director

Youth Pastor

Secretary

Other

Other

- -

HEARD THE LATEST?

☐ WEATHER
☐ SPORTS
☐ AUTO

| SEPTEMBER 24, 1996 | ANYTOWN | 50 CENTS |

ITEM:_____ SENT BY:_____ DATE:_____

Please read this within_____day(s), initial it, and pass it on to the next person. Return to_____by_____. Thanks!

NAME:	NAME:	NAME:	NAME:	NAME:
DEPARTMENT:	DEPARTMENT:	DEPARTMENT:	DEPARTMENT:	DEPARTMENT:

Comment on a separate sheet!

Makin' Tracks

Please read and initial this, then "make tracks" to pass it on. Thanks!

DESCRIPTION: _____

DATE SENT: _____

BY WHOM: _____ **RETURN BY:** _____

_____Pastor

_____Associate Pastor(s)

_____Music Director

_____Youth Pastor

_____Secretary

_____Other

_____Other

- -

When I Saw This...
I Thought of YOU!

ITEM:_____

DATE SENT:_____

BY WHOM: _____
Please take a look at this within_____day(s) and pass it on to the next person. Return to me by_____.

1.

2.

3.

4.

Count Me In!

Keep plenty of these forms on hand so you always have a ready pool of skilled volunteers. With these completed forms, you will know what talents you can tap, what experience you can benefit from, and who to go to for an enthusiastic hug!

Terrific Tips

Count Me In!

✔ Distribute forms to your entire congregation when you have "Children's Day" or a special recruitment drive.

✔ Keep a few forms in your day planner to have handy at a moment's notice. Casual conversations can lead to dedicated workers!

✔ Fold forms in thirds and stamp and address the back panels so people can fill out the forms at their leisure. Then they can simply mail them back to you.

✔ Make several photocopies of completed forms so you can file them by grade-level interest, skills or hobbies, and availability. Then, when you have a specific spot to fill, you can scan the appropriate files instead of searching through the whole stack.

Count Me In!

NAME:_____ PHONE NUMBER: _____

ADDRESS:_____

AGE:_____ I'VE BEEN A CHRISTIAN FOR... _____

I'D LIKE TO WORK WITH: (NUMBER IN ORDER OF PREFERENCE)

Nursery   3s and 4s   PreK/K   1st/2nd   3rd/4th   5th/6th

MY EXPERIENCE WITH CHILDREN:

SPECIAL SKILLS I'D LIKE TO SHARE:

I'M AVAILABLE:

Sunday school   Wednesday night

Sunday morning worship   Year round

Sunday evening worship   Summer

Other:

I'D LIKE TO:

Teach   Help with special events

Volunteer goods or services   Assist

Other:

REFERENCES:

Name: _____ Phone: _____

Name: _____ Phone: _____

Name: _____ Phone: _____

Who's Who in Our Church

Make visitors feel instantly at home or help new volunteers get acquainted with "those in the know" with this easy-to-update form. Just fill in the blanks and photocopy for distribution. Looking at the form will also help the kids in your care get an idea of how the church is organized.

Terrific Tips

Who's Who In Our Church

- ✔ Post photocopies of this form in conspicuous areas of your church.

- ✔ Enlarge the form and add photos to create a fun and informative bulletin board.

- ✔ Update this form immediately after church elections or staff changes.

- ✔ Add phone numbers and distribute this form to your committee chairpersons to facilitate their communication tasks.

Who's Who in Our Church

Pastor:

Associate Pastor(s):

Music Director:

Youth Director:

Children's Ministry Director:

Church Secretary:

Custodial Supervisor:

Chairman of the Board:

Others that make the church work:

Programs

For Women:

For Men:

For Teens:

For Children:

For Seniors:

Schedule of Services

Sunday school:

Sunday morning worship:

Sunday evening worship:

Midweek:

Regular Events:

Phone Friends

(People Who Can Help)

Quicker than dialing information. More fun than a phone book. Keep this form at your fingertips for fast and easy community resource reference. Whether you need to reserve a park facility for your annual picnic or submit a press release, look no further than this form.

Terrific Tips

Phone Friends

✔ If possible, include a name with every number to personalize your calls. Keep notes to remind you who has helped you in the past.

✔ Post this form near your desk so anyone acting in your stead will have easy access to often-called numbers.

✔ Adapt the list to fit your specific needs, then pass the numbers on as you delegate responsibilities.

Phone Friends

(People Who Can Help)

ORGANIZATION	CONTACT PERSON	PHONE #
Parks and recreation		
Local newspaper		
Other media publicity		
School district contact		
Police department		
Local government official(s)		
Bus service		
Food/clothing bank		
Other ministry workers		
Other		

Friendly Reminders

Keep your ministry's goals, prayer concerns, and agendas uppermost in your helpers' minds. Each of these reminder forms can be photocopied on card stock and sent through the mail for the price of a postcard! Use them frequently to remind your volunteers how important their support is to the children's ministry of your church.

Terrific Tips

Friendly Reminders

✔ Follow up each planning meeting with a postcard to remind team members that "People can make all kinds of plans, but only the Lord's plan will happen" (Proverbs 19:21).

✔ If you don't want to mail postcards, run these notices on bright colored paper and attach them to your attendance sheets.

✔ Enlarge either of these two forms to use as posters in your children's education department.

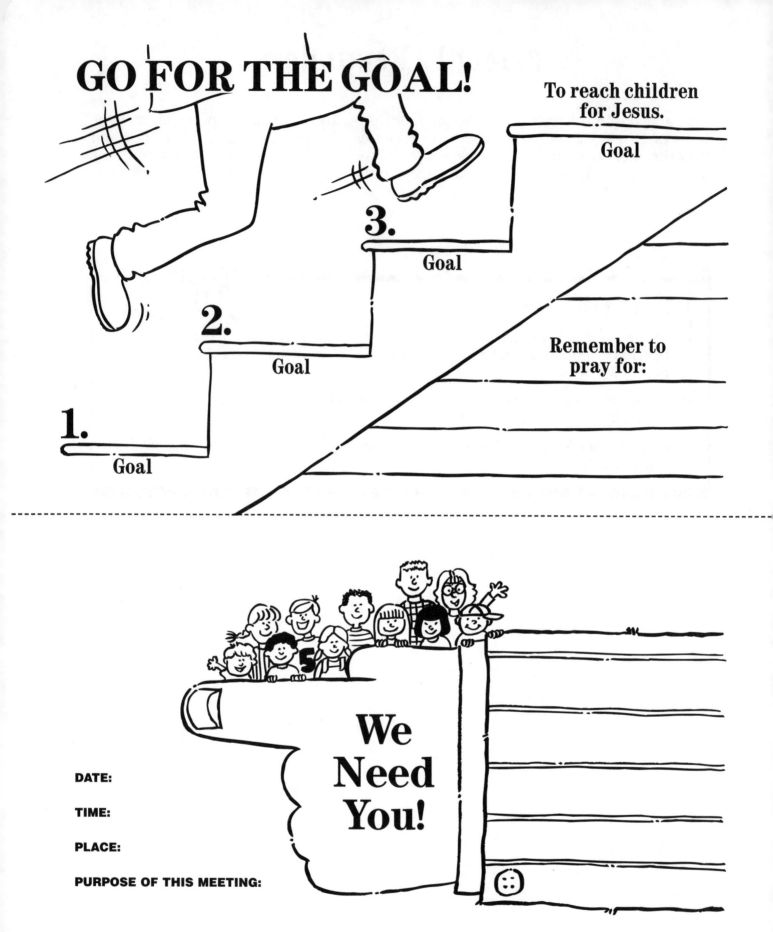

GO FOR THE GOAL!

To reach children for Jesus.

Goal

3.

Goal

2.

Goal

Remember to pray for:

1.

Goal

We Need You!

DATE:

TIME:

PLACE:

PURPOSE OF THIS MEETING:

Calendar Communication

Time—it's the critical element in any organizational plan. Use the following calendars to see each day, week, month, and year at a glance. You can use this page to fill in everything but the date, then photocopy once a week or month. File your calendars in a three-ring binder for easy use!

Terrific Tips

Calendar Communication

✔ Enlarge each calendar to fit into any other organizational planner.

✔ Distribute photocopies of your calendar at planning meetings to share your overview with others.

✔ Leave a photocopy with the church secretary and ask to have pertinent church dates filled in as they become scheduled.

✔ Promote prompt communication by posting your weekly and monthly calendars in a prominent place to let co-workers in on your schedule.

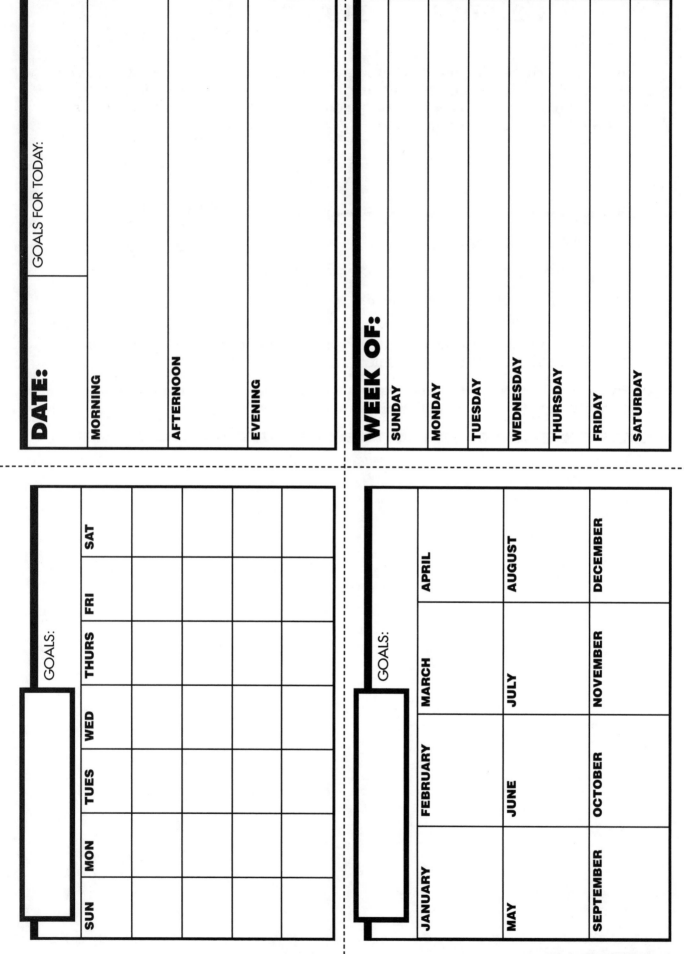

DATE:

GOALS FOR TODAY:

MORNING

AFTERNOON

EVENING

WEEK OF:

SUNDAY

MONDAY

TUESDAY

WEDNESDAY

THURSDAY

FRIDAY

SATURDAY

GOALS:

SUN	MON	TUES	WED	THURS	FRI	SAT

GOALS:

JANUARY	FEBRUARY	MARCH	APRIL
MAY	JUNE	JULY	AUGUST
SEPTEMBER	OCTOBER	NOVEMBER	DECEMBER

2

Administration Made Easy

It's easy to set lofty goals for yourself and your staff, but it's a tough job to reach those goals without administrative know-how. Don't let your ministry become mired in red tape. Use the forms in this chapter to keep accurate records, then use that information to make solid plans for the future. You'll be amazed at how easy organization can be by using these forms!

Touching Base

Hard to keep up with the new faces in your group? Have trouble keeping your schedule straight? Try this quick chart to help you stay in touch.

Terrific Tips

Touching Base

✔ Fill in the names and phone numbers of the students you'll be contacting (or make this a master list of everyone in your group).

✔ Make several photocopies of this form: one for home, one for church, and one for your day planner. You may want to post one by your phone, too.

✔ Under "Type" list what kind of contact you'll be making: N for note, V for visit, C for phone call, M for left message, and so on.

✔ Keep a running log. Jot down brief comments whenever you think about or talk to your students. Include ideas that will help you get to know your students better or follow up on any concerns.

✔ Pray for your students often.

Touching Base

NAME	PHONE #/ADDRESS	TYPE	DATE	COMMENTS

Roll Call

A class roster can be just another boring list OR it can be a valuable resource that helps you appreciate each child and helper in your class. Use the "creative space" on this form to personalize your roster to fit your particular needs.

Terrific Tips

Roll Call

✔ Use markers or colored pencils to draw attention to your list and to help everyone get to know each other better.

✔ Be sure to include your own name and the names of any helpers.

✔ Use the "Awesome Info" space to include special interests or talents, or even favorite foods, that will help you recognize each student's unique features. Make sure to include your own and your helper's "Awesome Info."

✔ Update the roster every few months and have students add "Awesome Info" in new categories (suggestions: favorite class, future plans, best gift, or favorite sport). See who can recall everyone's "Info" from previous updates.

✔ If you use this list to take attendance, be creative! Use small stickers between headings or use different colored highlighters to mark through first names one week, last names the next, and so on.

Roll Call

NAME	ADDRESS	AWESOME INFO

1 _____

2 _____

3 _____

4 _____

5 _____

6 _____

7 _____

8 _____

9 _____

10 _____

11 _____

12 _____

13 _____

14 _____

15 _____

16 _____

17 _____

18 _____

19 _____

20 _____

Keeping Track of Your Money

Don't let expenses get out of hand—take the mystery out of money management with these easy expense logs. Get in the habit of jotting down every expense on the general expense form and you'll find that finances no longer befuddle you.

Use the running expense form to keep track of regular expenses such as phone bills, equipment rental, and maintenance costs. That way, expenses that need to be submitted on a monthly or quarterly basis will be ready to go when the time comes.

Terrific Tips

General Expenses

✔ Keep expense logs handy in your classroom, automobile, checkbook, or by your phone.

✔ Make photocopies of expense logs on colored paper. (Green may be a good reminder for money.)

✔ Encourage your staff to be good stewards by getting into the habit of jotting down every expense.

✔ If you're not sure how to list an expense, list it in a way that's easy for you to remember.

Running Expenses

✔ Keep this form in a convenient place where you'll see it often.

✔ Attach the form to an envelope to hold receipts.

✔ Get in the habit of thinking ahead and jotting down expense possibilities as you plan your ministry.

✔ A clipboard offers a firm surface to write on and helps to keep your log from getting lost. You may want to hang it from a hook near your phone or by your desk.

$ $ $ General Expenses $ $ $

Name: _____

Organization or Group: _____

ITEM (NAME & DATE)	COST	PROJECT
$ $		
_____	_____	_____
_____	_____	_____
_____	_____	_____
_____	_____	_____
_____	_____	_____
_____	_____	_____
_____	_____	_____
_____	_____	_____

Total Expenses: _____   Today's Date: _____

Signature: _____

- -

Running Expenses

NAME:_____

DATES: _____   _____
         (From)   (To)

DATE	AMOUNT	ITEM DESCRIPTION & PROJECT

Signature _____

Rate Your Reaction

Get your kids' reactions to recent events with this easy-to-use questionnaire. It's important to keep questions simple and clear for children (and adults, too!). Allow "yes" and "no" answers where applicable. If you get a lot of negative responses, ask kids one-on-one for specific reasons why they didn't enjoy the activity.

Terrific Tips

Rate Your Reaction

✔ Photocopy forms on bright (neon-colored) paper.

✔ Be positive as you ask kids, parents, and leaders for their feedback.

✔ Be willing to hear negative comments about the event. Try not to take them personally—remember it's the event that's being evaluated, not you.

✔ Listen. If you ask for someone's opinion, take the time to listen seriously and consider his or her thoughts. Kids are wonderfully honest and have terrific ideas of their own.

✔ File evaluations with the other event/activity information for future reference. Review reaction ratings before planning another similar event.

Rate Your Reaction

	YES	NO
1. Did you like this activity?	_____	_____
2. Would you enjoy doing this again?	_____	_____
3. Would you invite a friend?	_____	_____
4. Did you meet someone new?	_____	_____
5. Was the cost reasonable?	_____	_____
6. Will you tell someone about it?	_____	_____
7. Did you learn something new about yourself?	_____	_____
8. Did you learn something new about God?	_____	_____
9. Did you get to know others in the group better?	_____	_____
10. Are you glad you came?	_____	_____

11. On a scale of 1 to 10, how would you rate this activity? _____

12. If you had to describe this activity in one word, what would it be? _____

13. What did you like best about this activity? _____

_____

_____

14. What would you change about the activity? _____

_____

_____

15. Why do you think we did this activity? _____

_____

_____

Publicity Checklist

Newsletters and posters are fun, informative ways to get the word out about your ministry.

A newsletter for children's ministry should be fun to read—and to write. Try to include children in the production of your newsletter. It's great training for them, and they'll offer a wealth of creative ideas for you. And remember—a newsletter is really about people, not just news.

Posters featuring bright colors and bold print catch attention and build excitement. Brief and very specific information makes details easy to remember. Use the poster checklist to organize your thoughts, count your costs, and make sure your posters are picture perfect.

Terrific Tips

Read All About It!

✔ Use lots of names and photographs.

✔ Cartoons add a lot of enjoyment for kids (and adults!).

✔ Photocopy your newsletter on colored paper.

✔ Gear your newsletter to your audience, whether it be co-workers, parents, or the kids themselves. Use large, bold letters and lots of pictures for the children's portions.

✔ If something doesn't work in an issue, change it for the next edition.

Perfect Posters

✔ Get excited about your event. Your enthusiasm will show.

✔ Do something different or unusual—write backward and place the poster opposite a mirror, cut letters out of wallpaper or fabric, or hang posters from ceilings or stair rails.

✔ Keep the writing simple, so children can read or help create the poster.

✔ Use drawings, photos, cartoons, or clip art to get your message across. Consider bold/contrasting colors such as purple and orange or bright blue and yellow.

Read All About It!

Group Name:_____

Newsletter Title: _____

Print Date: _____

Articles to include:

TITLE: _____**WRITER:** _____**DUE BY:** _____

TITLE: _____**WRITER:** _____**DUE BY:** _____

TITLE: _____**WRITER:** _____**DUE BY:** _____

Photos to include:

PHOTO: _____**PHOTOGRAPHER:** _____**DUE BY:** _____

PHOTO: _____**PHOTOGRAPHER:** _____**DUE BY:** _____

PHOTO: _____**PHOTOGRAPHER:** _____**DUE BY:** _____

Proofread by: _____

Addressed or mailed by: _____

Perfect Posters

Check off the following items as you complete them:

_____Event Title/Headline

_____Detail information for poster (attach separate sheet)

_____Number of posters needed

_____Cartoons/Clip Art

_____Sketch of poster

_____Double-check details and spelling for accuracy

_____Finish date of poster

_____Display location(s)

_____Remove poster after event (file for future reference)

Expressions From the Heart

Everyone likes to feel appreciated. A few words go a long way to help children (or anyone, for that matter) feel loved and valued. A short note sent in the mail or delivered personally can make all the difference in how others view themselves and their efforts. Use these forms to help you get in the habit of expressing your thanks and encouragment.

Terrific Tips

Many Thanks!

✔ Let your "thank you" come from your heart.

✔ Just do it. There will never be the "perfect" time to sit down and write those notes. Try to write to everyone in your group during the course of a year.

✔ Ask God to guide you in composing your message.

✔ Add colors and your own style to the "form letter." Include stickers, balloons, bookmarks, or a coupon for a hug or high five.

✔ Personalize each note by saying something particular about the person. For example, "I saw the way you helped Karen put the puzzles away. You're so kind. Thank you!"

✔ Adapt this form to recognize co-workers and volunteers, also.

Plenty of Praise

✔ Pray for your students often. Writing a short note of appreciation will flow from time well-spent in prayer.

✔ Find out your students' interests and hobbies. Then be genuine with your praise.

✔ Get involved with parents so they feel comfortable letting you know when their child could use a word of encouragement.

✔ Make sure to recognize co-workers and volunteers, too.

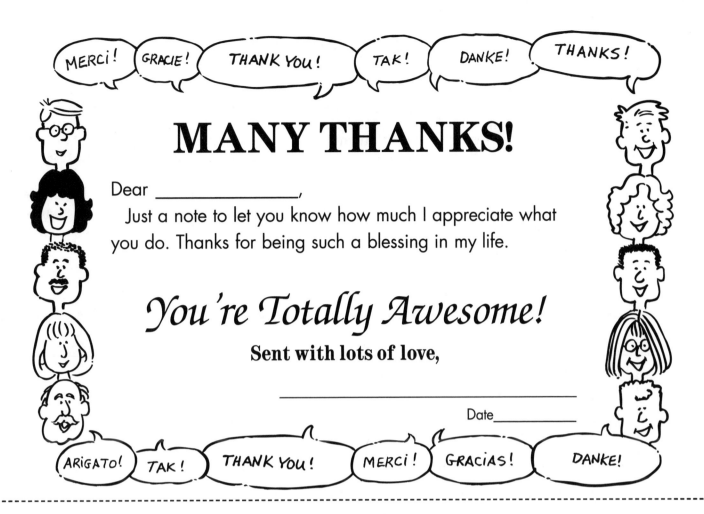

MANY THANKS!

Dear _____,

Just a note to let you know how much I appreciate what you do. Thanks for being such a blessing in my life.

You're Totally Awesome!

Sent with lots of love,

_____

Date_____

(Speech bubbles: MERCI! GRACIE! THANK YOU! TAK! DANKE! THANKS! ARIGATO! TAK! THANK YOU! MERCI! GRACIAS! DANKE!)

Plenty of Praise

Dear _____,

You deserve a round of applause because

☐ I'M GLAD I KNOW YOU!

☐ YOU'RE VERY SPECIAL!

☐ IT'S FUN TO BE WITH YOU!

☐ I'M PROUD OF YOU!

☐ I LIKE YOU!

☐ YOU'RE WONDERFUL!

☐ ALL OF THE ABOVE!

Love,_____

Put It in Print

There's power in the pen, they say. Whether you want to publish your own information or use already published material, these forms will help guide your steps.

It's not just a courtesy to request permission to copy material, it's also the law. Use the following Copyright Permission request form when you want to use published material.

And when you write your own information, remember—publicity equals people! You're well on your way toward a successful event when you let lots of people know about it. A well-written news release is the surest way to get the news out.

Terrific Tips

Copyright Permission

✔ Be sure your information in the letter is accurate (correct address, dates you want to use the material, and how you plan to use it).

✔ Give yourself plenty of time to receive a return response. Four to six weeks is usually enough.

✔ Understand that in some cases there may be a charge for using the material.

✔ Include your phone number (or the church office number) in case there's a question that can be handled with a phone call.

Sample Press Release

✔ Newspapers operate on inflexible schedules, so be sure to deliver your press release on time. Call your local newspaper(s) to double-check deadlines.

✔ Type and double-space the press release and be sure to include your name and phone number.

✔ Don't be wordy. Include only pertinent information about your event—the newspaper editor will cut out the fluff, anyway.

✔ Include a nonreturnable black-and-white photo (with identifying names and information on the back) or ask the newspaper to send a photographer to your event.

Copyright Permission

Name:

Address:

Phone: (   )

Date:

Copyright Owner:

Address:

Attn.: Rights and Permissions

Dear _____,

   My name is_____, and I am a part of the children's ministry

at_____. Recently I enjoyed hearing/reading _____.

I would like to request permission to use the material _____

on page _____for our _____. We plan to make _____ copies.

There will be no charge for copies made.

   Thank you for your attention in this matter. Please let me hear from you if you have questions or

need additional information. I will anticipate hearing from you in regard to permission status, credit

line, and any expected fee.

Sincerely,

_____

Sample Press Release

FOR IMMEDIATE RELEASE

Date:_____

Church: _____

Contact person: _____

Phone: _____

Event: _____

Date of event: _____

Desert Springs Bible Church will host a carnival for children of all ages on Saturday, March 18, from 10 a.m. to 3 p.m. on the church grounds. The carnival will feature rides, food, face painting, sack races, prizes, and much more.

The event is free and open to the public. Donations will be used to purchase playground equipment for Desert Springs Christian Preschool.

Desert Springs Bible Church is located at 16215 N. Spring St., Hatboro. For more information, call 555-5000.

Ready Requests

Refund request forms are wonderful tools for heading off snags in a smooth-running ministry. For example, even the best of planners will sometimes incur out-of-pocket expenses for church programs. Keep accurate records and speed up the reimbursement process with this simple Refund Request form.

And nothing brings an activity to a halt like running short on materials. Stay ahead of the game and stock your shelves the easy way—give this Supply Request form to all your teachers. Collect the forms, and you've got your shopping list. What could be simpler?

Terrific Tips

Refund Request

✔ Always include your original receipt for the expense. Keep a photocopy for your own files.

✔ Keep photocopies of the form handy in your car or at home.

✔ Fill out a refund request as soon after your purchase as possible—it's easy to forget those little expenses, but they do add up.

✔ Check with the financial director of your church to find out how often to submit refund requests (monthly or as they occur) and when to expect a refund.

Supply Request

✔ Plan ahead. Don't wait until Saturday to plan for Sunday's activities.

✔ Make your requests specific. State the quantity, size, and brand, if applicable, of each item you need.

✔ Keep forms in classrooms and encourage teachers to take a few home.

Refund Request

Requested by: _____ Date: _____

Purchase item: _____

Date of purchase: _____

Method of payment: _____

Receipt attached? _____

Reason for purchase: _____

_____

Signature: _____

Supply Request

Name: _____ Date: _____

Class or Group: _____

Date needed: _____

Item needed: _____

Size: _____ Quantity: _____

Color(s): _____ Brand: _____

Special instructions: _____

_____

Item needed: _____

Size: _____ Quantity: _____

Color(s): _____ Brand: _____

Special instructions: _____

_____

Signature: _____

Classroom Communications

The 12 forms in this chapter are designed to make your classroom a fun and fruitful place to be. No more will guesswork and last-minute planning dominate. Document, instead! Get to know your students better and help them know you! Know which songs and games you used last month and which ones are waiting in the wings. Keep parents informed of upcoming lessons and student progress. Use these forms to streamline your classroom communications and to make more time for your ministry!

What I Like

Let your kids know how important they are by showing an interest in their lives. Use this form to find out more about their likes and dislikes. Older kids can fill out the forms themselves, while younger kids will enjoy drawing picture responses as you read the questions aloud. Let your discoveries help you plan activities tailored specifically to your kids.

Terrific Tips

What I Like

- ✔ Use this "kid survey" as an icebreaker during the first class session or to welcome new kids to the group.

- ✔ Share information from the survey with fellow teachers; help them become familiar with the interests of each child.

- ✔ Consider using an instant-print camera to take pictures of your kids to attach to their surveys.

- ✔ Be sure to fill out a form yourself! Sharing about yourself will help kids feel closer to you.

WHAT i LiKE

Hi! My name is_____.

I'm _____ years old. My favorite color is _____.

My favorite food is_____.

My pet is a_____named _____.

My favorite subject in school is _____.

The sport I like best is _____.

One thing I'd like to ask God is _____

_____.

DURiNG CLASS TiME i'D LiKE TO...

	Never				Sometimes				Always	
play games	1	2	3	4	5	6	7	8	9	10
act out a Bible story	1	2	3	4	5	6	7	8	9	10
use puppets	1	2	3	4	5	6	7	8	9	10
make crafts	1	2	3	4	5	6	7	8	9	10
draw pictures	1	2	3	4	5	6	7	8	9	10
sing songs	1	2	3	4	5	6	7	8	9	10
read books	1	2	3	4	5	6	7	8	9	10
watch a movie	1	2	3	4	5	6	7	8	9	10
listen to a tape	1	2	3	4	5	6	7	8	9	10

Who Am I?

This form provides a great way to introduce yourself to your kids' parents and to answer their questions before they're asked. Parents will value this convenient Who Am I? form and will applaud your professionalism and personable spirit.

Terrific Tips

Who Am I?

✔ Use this form at the beginning of the year to introduce yourself and your teachers. Keep extra photocopies on hand for new students.

✔ Place a small photo of yourself in the corner of the form to help parents identify you.

✔ Encourage each of your helpers and co-workers to complete a form as well. You may even want to post the completed forms on the church bulletin board.

Who Am I?

Place photo here

_____
Name

_____
Title

_____
Class

Address: _____ Phone: _____

_____ Occupation: _____

I chose to teach this class because: _____

_____

_____

My teaching goals for your child are: _____

_____

_____

Teaching experience: _____

_____

Hobbies: _____

_____

Other interests: _____

_____

_____

_____

Student Information

Keeping a master file on every student doesn't have to be a daunting task. Just have parents fill out a Student Information form for each of their children, then file the forms in a central location. You and members of your staff will always know where to look for important phone numbers, medical information, and other vital facts.

Terrific Tips

Student Information

✔ Keep photocopies of completed Student Information forms in a note-book and carry the notebook with you on class trips or retreats.

✔ Let teachers and administrative staff know where completed forms are kept. Perhaps your church office could accommodate these master files.

✔ Update the information annually. Be sure to have the parents of new students fill out the forms to add to your master file. Then just add photocopies to your notebook.

Student Information

Class_____

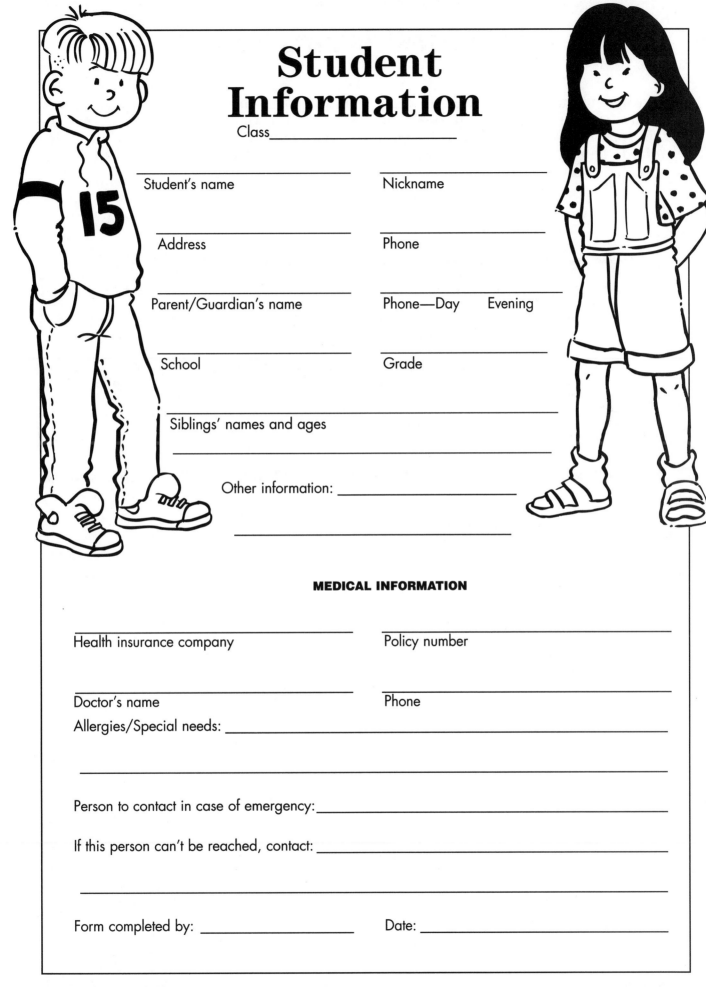

Student's name _____   Nickname _____

Address _____   Phone _____

Parent/Guardian's name _____   Phone—Day   Evening _____

School _____   Grade _____

Siblings' names and ages _____

Other information: _____

_____

MEDICAL INFORMATION

Health insurance company _____   Policy number _____

Doctor's name _____   Phone _____

Allergies/Special needs: _____

_____

Person to contact in case of emergency:_____

If this person can't be reached, contact: _____

_____

Form completed by: _____   Date: _____

Student Progress Report

Keep parents up-to-date about their child's progress in your class with this quick and easy form. Simply fill in the top portion of the form, and you're ready to run photocopies for the entire class. Personalize the bottom half of the form by filling in the child's name and circling your comments. Be sure to add a personal note in the comment section of each form.

Terrific Tips

Student Progress Report

✔ Use Student Progress forms after each unit or quarter to affirm children or to share concerns with parents.

✔ Have extra photocopies on hand to use when a child needs special praise or if a behavior problem arises. Just fill out the form before the end of class and give it to the parent after class.

✔ Make photocopies of completed forms. Keep copies in the child's folder for future reference.

STUDENT PROGRESS REPORT

_____
Church name

_____
Date

_____
Class

DEAR PARENT:

I'm so glad to have _____ in my class. We've been learning about

_____ during the last unit/quarter. One thing I've noticed about your

child is _____.

Thank you for the opportunity to share God's love with your child.

_____
Name

	ALWAYS	SOMETIMES	NEEDS WORK
Works well with others	☐	☐	☐
Is considerate of others	☐	☐	☐
Listens well	☐	☐	☐
Is a good helper	☐	☐	☐
Follows directions	☐	☐	☐

Other comments, praises, concerns: _____

_____

_____

_____
Teacher(s)

_____
Date

Meeting Guide

What topics should I teach? What supplies do I need? Will I need any special helpers or equipment? Answer these questions and more with this helpful Meeting Guide form.

Terrific Tips

Meeting Guide

✔ Use this form to plan not only class time, but special gatherings, retreat sessions, and Bible studies as well.

✔ Be sure to state the purpose of your meeting, then support that purpose with every part of your plan.

✔ Double-check. Go over your plan to make sure that every activity, game, or craft teaches the kids about the lesson's goal.

✔ Make photocopies of the Meeting Guide form for your helpers. Go over their assignments and have them highlight their responsibilities on their forms.

Meeting Guide

Meeting/Event: _____

Date: _____ Time: _____

Location: _____

Lesson goal: _____

_____

Scripture reference: _____

Games planned: _____

Snacks planned: _____

Crafts planned: _____

Music planned: _____

Supplies needed: _____

Equipment needed: _____

Transportation needed: _____

    Parent permission forms:_____

    Medical release forms: _____

Comments: _____

_____

_____

Instant Evaluations

Let experience be your guide with these quick evaluation forms. Let kids rate their reactions to trips, activities, games, or even snacks. Use the Instant Evaluation forms any time you want kids' immediate reactions to an activity. You'll get to know your kids better and planning will be a snap with the insights you gain. There are two forms, one geared for older kids and one for the younger crowd.

Terrific Tips

Instant Evaluations

✔ Use these forms as soon after an event as possible, before reactions fade. Encourage discussion with questions such as "Why did you like this game?" or "What would have made this trip more fun?" Make notes of kids' comments.

✔ Share your kids' ratings with fellow teachers and administrators.

✔ Staple ratings together and keep them on file to guide you in future planning.

✔ Don't take negative ratings personally. Remember—kids are rating experiences, not you.

Instant Evaluation

Group: _____ Date: _____

Activity: _____

Date of activity: _____

Color the face that shows how you felt about this activity.

Group: _____ Date: _____

Activity: _____

Date of activity: _____

My Evaluation

Supply Checklist

A request form is a real timesaver for leaders. Simply check the items needed and return to the appropriate staff person. Or use the form as a shopping list for classroom materials or trips. All you need is this form and a pencil for instant organization.

Terrific Tips

Supply Checklist

✔ Give a copy of the list to each teacher and compile the totals for your classroom needs.

✔ Encourage teachers to clip coupons for items they need and turn the coupons in with their request forms.

✔ Make parents aware of classroom needs by giving them the request list with the needed items circled or highlighted.

✔ Clip off the list of media needs to give to the appropriate staff person.

Supply Checklist

Name _____   Phone _____
Class _____   Needed by _____

CHALK
Sidewalk _____
Regular_____

CONSTRUCTION PAPER
Size_____
Color(s)_____

PAPER
Size _____
Color(s) _____
Manila _____
Newsprint _____
Typing _____
Butcher _____

POSTER BOARD
White_____
Color(s) _____

CRAYONS
Regular _____
Large _____

MARKERS
Fine tip _____
Broad tip _____

GLUE
Sticks _____
White_____

Other _____

PAINT
Tempera colors _____
Watercolor_____

BRUSHES
Easel_____
Sponge_____

YARN
Color(s) _____

TAPE
Transparent _____
Masking_____

Other _____

MEDIA NEEDS
TV/VCR _____
Videocassette Recorder ____
Videotape _____
Camera _____
Cassette Player _____

Film _____

Other _____

_____

PARENTS: PLEASE HELP US IN COLLECTING THE FOLLOWING ITEMS.

Shoe boxes _____   Egg cartons_____   Butter tubs _____
Baby jars _____   Magazines _____   Boxes (size)_____

Other _____

I've Got a Great Idea!

Kids are full of creative ideas and love to share what they think. Make the most of their creativity by providing a Suggestion Box in your classroom. Encourage children to make suggestions about games, crafts, activities, ways to share what they learn with others, or anything else that's on their minds. Let parents and other adults submit suggestions, as well.

Terrific Tips

I've Got a Great Idea!

✔ Pick a special place in the room to put the suggestion forms, pencils, and the Suggestion Box. Take time to explain to the kids the importance of their ideas and tell them you're looking forward to reading their suggestions.

✔ Tell kids they don't need to put their names on the suggestions unless they want to.

✔ Share the suggestions you receive with the class and encourage class discussion.

✔ When possible, put kids' ideas to use. Praise your students for their input.

✔ Keep suggestions on file and use them during planning meetings as springboards for new games, crafts, and activities.

Here's My Great Idea!

CRAFT?   GAME?   ACTIVITY?   WAY TO SHARE?

I'VE GOT A GREAT IDEA!

_____
_____
_____
_____
_____
_____
Signed

- -

I've Got a Cool Idea!!!

Game?_____
_____

Craft?_____
_____

Activity?_____
_____

Way to share?_____
_____

Other?_____
_____

_____
Signed

Record-Breaking Records

With the next two forms, you'll always know where you've been and where you're going.

Have you found yourself thinking, "How did we teach this last time?" "Have I used this before?" or "The kids really like this; I need to remember it for the future." Keep track of your lesson plans by using the efficient Lesson Diary form.

The What's Coming Up form is a great way to keep parents up-to-date and to get them involved in what you're teaching! The form lets parents know the specifics of what their children will be learning and gives suggestions for supplementing these lessons at home.

Terrific Tips

Lesson Diary

✔ Use a notebook with dividers to separate units of study. Then complete and file a Lesson Diary form for each lesson. Highlight activities the kids' really enjoyed, and note ideas to improve other activities.

✔ Refer to the Lesson Diary when planning for a new year or a new unit. Revise ideas with each use.

✔ When the time comes for you to move to a new teaching position, leave a copy of the Lesson Diary for the new leader or teacher.

What's Coming Up

✔ Complete this form at the beginning of each unit and make photocopies to hand out to parents at the first class or to send home with kids. You may want to call a parent meeting for each new unit and give parents photocopies of the form.

✔ Make a paper kite to display in your classroom and write the titles of upcoming lessons on the kite's tail. That way parents and older kids can tell at a glance what's coming up.

✔ Make suggestions for fun family activities that support unit lessons. Be sure to include the main idea and Scripture reference of each lesson and suggest activities that will not only enhance the lesson, but will provide opportunities for family growth and sharing.

Lesson Diary

Class: _____

Unit: _____   Date used: _____

Lesson: _____

Scripture passage: _____

Lesson goal(s): _____

_____

Game: _____

   Supplies: _____

Game: _____

   Supplies: _____

Craft: _____

   Supplies: _____

Craft: _____

   Supplies: _____

Puzzles: _____

Music: _____

Media: TV/VCR _____   Videotape _____

   Cassette player _____   Cassette _____

   Other _____

Books: _____

Guest speaker: _____

Snack: _____

Special items: _____

Comments: _____

_____

_____

_____

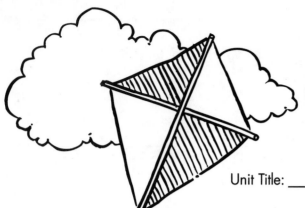

What's Coming Up

Here are some highlights of our next unit of study.

Unit Title: _____

Lesson 1: _____

_____

Lesson 2: _____

_____

Lesson 3: _____

_____

Lesson 4: _____

_____

For Family Fun

Use the following family fun ideas to augment the lessons your child is studying.

Lesson 1 Activity: _____

_____

Lesson 2 Activity: _____

_____

Lesson 3 Activity: _____

_____

Lesson 4 Activity: _____

_____

NO-WORK PAPERWORK

4
Parent Pleasers

Parents want, and need, to stay informed about their children. They want to know what their children are being taught, how they're being taught, and by whom they're being taught. Keeping parents informed is not only a responsibility, it's a wonderful opportunity! When parents are involved, they can add needed support, share concerns, and reinforce lessons at home. Let the following forms help you to work with parents to strengthen the faith of the students you teach.

Calling All Kids

Communicating with your kids and their parents is vital to a successful ministry. The fastest, most efficient way to get information to your group is to use the Calling Chain form. Simply call the chain leaders, give them your message, and have them call the first person on their lists. Each person will then call the next person on the list. For accuracy, encourage everyone in the chain to write down the message and repeat it back to the caller.

The families in your ministry may want to contact each other, too. They may have questions about upcoming events at church, or maybe they'd just like to touch base with each other. And the kids in your class often form friendships that would thrive outside of church. Use the handy Class Directory to encourage Christian fun and fellowship outside the classroom, too!

Terrific Tips

Calling Chain

✔ Complete the Calling Chain form and make a copy for each chain member as well as a copy for your church files.

✔ Update the Calling Chain form regularly as class rosters change.

✔ Ask chain members when would be the most convenient time to call, then record that information on the form.

Class Directory

✔ Make multiple photocopies of the completed Class Directory to give to teachers and church staff.

✔ Laminate a copy to keep by your phone for easy access.

✔ Update your Class Directory regularly. Then pass the new information on to parents and families.

Calling Chain

Directions: Please call the next person on your list, repeat the message, and ask that person to pass the word. If you are unable to reach the next person on the list, keep the chain going by skipping to the following person. Try later to reach the person you skipped and let your chain leader know if you are unsuccessful. Thanks!

CHAIN LEADER:	PHONE:	BEST TIME TO CALL
Name:	Phone:	
Name:	Phone:	
Name:	Phone:	
Name:	Phone:	
Name:	Phone:	

CHAIN LEADER:	PHONE:	
Name:	Phone:	
Name:	Phone:	
Name:	Phone:	
Name:	Phone:	
Name:	Phone:	

CHAIN LEADER:	PHONE:	
Name:	Phone:	
Name:	Phone:	
Name:	Phone:	
Name:	Phone:	
Name:	Phone:	

CHAIN LEADER:	PHONE:	
Name:	Phone:	
Name:	Phone:	
Name:	Phone:	
Name:	Phone:	
Name:	Phone:	

Class Directory

CLASS LEADER: _____   CLASS: _____

PHONE: _____   DATE: _____

CHILDREN

NAME: _____   NAME: _____

PARENT: _____   PARENT: _____

ADDRESS: _____   ADDRESS: _____

_____   _____

PHONE: _____   PHONE: _____

NAME: _____   NAME: _____

PARENT: _____   PARENT: _____

ADDRESS: _____   ADDRESS: _____

_____   _____

PHONE: _____   PHONE: _____

NAME: _____   NAME: _____

PARENT: _____   PARENT: _____

ADDRESS: _____   ADDRESS: _____

_____   _____

PHONE: _____   PHONE: _____

NAME: _____   NAME: _____

PARENT: _____   PARENT: _____

ADDRESS: _____   ADDRESS: _____

_____   _____

PHONE: _____   PHONE: _____

NAME: _____   NAME: _____

PARENT: _____   PARENT: _____

ADDRESS: _____   ADDRESS: _____

_____   _____

PHONE: _____   PHONE: _____

Parent Calendar

A monthly calendar is a super way to keep parents and kids informed about upcoming activities. On the appropriate days, list the upcoming activities, times, and locations. If space allows, also include the contact person's name and phone number.

Terrific Tips

Parent Calendar

✔ Spruce up your calendar by including birthdays of kids and teachers. Add trivia questions about Bible stories you've covered or include riddles about upcoming lessons. Be creative!

✔ Involve your kids in making the calendar by letting them draw illustrations for upcoming events or Bible stories. Use a photocopier to reduce their drawings to a size usable on the calendar.

✔ Make your calendar a complete source of information (one that will stay on the refrigerator!) by listing important church events and holidays.

✔ Mail your calendar with newsletters to ensure that every family gets one. Post your calendar in the classroom and on bulletin boards in the church, and keep extra photocopies in the classroom or church office.

Parent Calendar

SUNDAY	MONDAY	TUESDAY	WEDNESDAY	THURSDAY	FRIDAY	SATURDAY

Parent Information

Your kids' parents or guardians can be an untapped source of help and support in the classroom. Finding out more about your kids' parents will not only help you create a special bond with them, but will afford a real chance to involve them in their children's spiritual growth.

Terrific Tips

Parent Information

✔ Let parents know that the information they give will be kept confidential. Only you and your staff need to be aware of the information given on the Parent Information form.

✔ Update your information each year. If possible, attach a picture of the family on the form.

✔ Ask parents to complete the form during the first parent meeting of the year. Keep forms on hand for parents who don't attend the meeting. Ask them to take a moment to fill out the form at a more convenient time.

✔ Often a parent would love to volunteer his or her talents, but is just waiting for an invitation. Make the first move with this easy form.

Parent Information

Child's Name: _____ Phone: _____

Mother's Name: _____

Workplace: _____ Phone: _____

Hobbies, Interests, Sports: _____

_____

Father's Name: _____

Workplace: _____ Phone: _____

Hobbies, Interests, Sports: _____

_____

Guardian (if applicable): _____

Workplace: _____ Phone: _____

Hobbies, Interests, Sports: _____

_____

Marital Status:

___ Married   ___ Separated

___ Divorced   ___ Widowed

Favorite Family Activities:_____

Special Talents or Interests I'd Like to Share:_____

_____

Times That I'm Available to Volunteer: _____

Parent Newsletter Headings

Don't use the same boring style each time you communicate with parents. Catch their attention with these slick newsletter headings. By using these eye-catching headings, you reduce the chance of letters winding up in the trash before they're read!

Terrific Tips

Parent Newsletter Headings

✔ Reflect changes in season and highlight holidays with your headings.

✔ Keep a variety of headings on file to avoid boring reruns.

✔ Make your newsletters "keepers" by adding fun information like recipes, craft instructions, or suggestions for family activities.

PARENT NEWSLETTER HEADINGS

ESPECIALLY FOR ☆ PARENTS ☆

WARNING:
Reading This Newsletter May Be Advantageous to Your Spiritual Health.

STOP **DON'T READ THIS!!** *
*UNLESS YOU WANT YOUR KID TO GLOW AND GROW IN GOD.

Parent Survey

What do parents want their kids to learn in your class? What spiritual objectives are most important to them? Here's a simple way to find out. Use the Parent Survey form to ask parents about their goals for their kids. Their answers can offer valuable insights and be of great help in making lesson plans.

Terrific Tips

Parent Survey

✔ Customize the form to include other questions of interest to you. Simply add your questions to the end of the form.

✔ Use the form at the beginning of the year to help in planning your curriculum. Review completed forms with your staff and brainstorm ways to incorporate parents' goals into your own class objectives.

✔ Affirm parents for sharing their ideas and goals. Let them know that you appreciate their team effort in planning a spiritual path for their kids.

Parent Survey

1. What do you feel is most important for your child to learn in our class during the next year? Please circle your answers.

	LEAST IMPORTANT			MOST IMPORTANT	
Understanding who God is	1	2	3	4	5
Recognizing Jesus as God's Son	1	2	3	4	5
Learning Bible stories	1	2	3	4	5
Memorizing Scripture	1	2	3	4	5
Memorizing books of the Bible	1	2	3	4	5
Learning the Ten Commandments	1	2	3	4	5
Learning about prayer	1	2	3	4	5
Learning about our denomination	1	2	3	4	5
Sharing/Showing concern for others	1	2	3	4	5

2. What do you feel is the best way for your child to learn?

_____Hearing Bible stories and lessons

_____Seeing pictures or viewing videos

_____Crafts and games that support the lesson

3. How do you think we can best teach your child? _____

_____

_____

4. Are our meeting days/times convenient for your family? Yes _____   No_____

Comments: _____

_____

Before and After the Trip

Don't go anywhere without it! What is "it"? The signed permission form! Leaders and teachers run a serious risk if they take a child on a trip without a parent's permission. Use the top of the form to give parents all the information they need about upcoming trips. Then all you need is a parent or guardian's signature, and you're ready to go!

NOTE: Do not rely solely on permission forms to protect yourself and your church legally. For legal questions and concerns, consult an attorney.

Then after your trip, or any other event, make it easy for parents to share their ideas and opinions with you. Put a Suggestion Box by your classroom door. Also supply pencils and extra copies of the Suggestion Box form. Be sure to check the box after each class meeting.

Terrific Tips

Permission Please

✔ Make sure parents have signed and returned the forms to you well in advance of the trip. Use newsletters and class calendars to publicize the trip.

✔ In addition to signing the permission form, be sure to have parents fill out a Liability/Medical Release form on page 84.

✔ If there are any changes in transportation, time, or destination of the trip, communicate those changes immediately to the parents.

Suggestion Box

✔ Point out the box to parents and encourage their input. Let parents know their input can be anonymous.

✔ Share the new ideas from parents with your teachers, and use parent suggestions whenever possible.

✔ Affirm parents for taking the time to share their ideas.

Permission Please

My child, _____, has my permission to go

to_____on _____with his/her church class.

We'll leave the church at _____ and return at _____.

Transportation will be provided by _____.

_____
Parent/Guardian's Signature   Date

I would like to be a sponsor: Yes___   No___

Suggestion Box

_____
Name (Optional)

NO-WORK PAPERWORK

Introducing...Me!

Introduce yourself to parents by using this leader information form. You'll build trust and open the door to communication as you share basic information about yourself and your interests.

Introducing...Me!

Terrific Tips

✔ Use this form at the beginning of the year to introduce yourself to parents. You can give photocopies to parents on the first day of class or during the first parent meeting.

✔ Attach a photo of yourself in the corner of the form so parents will be able to easily recognize you. Or show your sense of humor by drawing a fun picture of yourself.

✔ White out information blanks that don't apply to you and add information that you feel is important or fun.

Introducing ... ME!

Name:_____

Class: _____

Phone: _____

Occupation: _____

FAMILY INFORMATION

Spouse: _____

Children and ages: _____

Hobbies, Interests, Sports: _____

_____

I chose to lead this class because _____

_____

Other teaching experience includes_____

_____

My teaching goals for your child are _____

_____

Nursery Sign-Ins

Parents want to know that their wee ones receive the best care possible. Have parents use Nursery Sign-In forms to specify their child's needs. This form will not only help you take great care of the children in your nursery, but will also help locate parents should the need arise.

Terrific Tips

Nursery Sign-Ins

✔ Make photocopies of the form and place copies on a clipboard, one (or more) for each room in the nursery.

✔ Instruct nursery workers to have every parent sign in before leaving a child in their care. Be sure parents fill in all of the information requested.

✔ Be sure all items coming in with the child (diaper bag, bottles, pacifiers, etc.) are labeled with the child's name.

Nursery Sign-Ins

Room: _____   Date: _____

Child's name: _____ Parent/Guardian's name: _____

Where parent(s) will be: _____

Special directions: _____

   Feeding needs: _____

   Feeding time: _____

   Nap time: _____

   Allergies: _____

   Special Needs: _____

Child's name: _____ Parent/Guardian's name: _____

Where parent(s) will be: _____

Special directions: _____

   Feeding needs: _____

   Feeding time: _____

   Nap time: _____

   Allergies: _____

   Special Needs: _____

Child's name: _____ Parent/Guardian's name: _____

Where parent(s) will be: _____

Special directions: _____

   Feeding needs: _____

   Feeding time: _____

   Nap time: _____

   Allergies: _____

   Special Needs: _____

Liability/Medical Release

Cover all the bases when planning for trips or retreats. Make sure parents complete and turn in this Liability/Medical Release form. Why is this form so important? The Liability/Medical Release form may protect you and the church from some liability claims. The form also authorizes adults in the organization to obtain emergency medical treatment for children in their care. The form further clarifies parent financial responsibility for any medical expenses incurred.

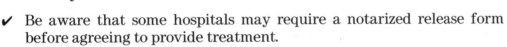

Liability/Medical Release

✔ Be aware that some hospitals may require a notarized release form before agreeing to provide treatment.

✔ Meet with parents before trips or retreats. Provide parents with photocopies of this form as well as a complete description of the trip or retreat, including: name and phone number of the trip leader, date and time of the trip, address and phone number of the destination, means of transportation, and names of adults sponsoring the trip.

✔ Be prepared to answer parents' questions. The Liability/Medical Release form is a legal document that may require some explanation from you. As part of your explanation, you can reassure parents that this is a standard form used by schools and churches in planning trips.

✔ Be sure to keep the forms in a notebook or binder to carry with you on the trip. You will need them in case of an emergency.

Liability/Medical Release

RELEASE OF ALL CLAIMS

In consideration for being accepted by _____ for
(Name of Church)

participation in _____, we, being the parent(s) or legal
(Name of trip or activity)

guardian(s) of _____, do release and agree to hold harmless
(Name of child)

_____ and the director thereof from any and all liability,
(Name of Church)

claims, or demands for personal injury, as well as damage and expenses, of any nature that may be incurred by the parent/guardian and child-participant that occur while the child is participating in the above described trip or activity.

We, on the behalf of our child-participant, assume all risk of personal injury, damage, and expense as the result of participation in recreational activities involved.

Authorization and permission are given to said church to furnish any necessary transportation, food, and lodging for our child-participant.

We, as parents/legal guardians of the child-participant, give our permission for him/her to participate fully in the trip/activity. We give our permission to take said participant to a doctor or hospital and authorize medical treatment, including but not in limitation to emergency surgery or medical treatment, and assume the responsibility of all medical bills, if any. We understand that we will be contacted if at all possible and that our family physician will be contacted if possible, but in the event that he/she cannot be reached, the minister/trip leader may choose a reputable physician.

Should it be necessary for the participant to return home due to medical reasons, disciplinary action, or otherwise, we assume all transportation costs.

_____
Name of child

_____   _____
Father   Date   Mother   Date
(Both parents must sign, unless parents are separated or divorced in which case the custodial parent must sign.)

_____   _____
Parent(s) Phone   Date

_____
Legal Guardian

_____
Guardian's Phone

_____
Pastor's Phone

Hospital Insurance _____Yes _____No   _____
Insurance Company _____   Notary   Date

_____   _____
Policy Number   Physician
Emergency phone numbers

_____

_____

From the Heart

Deep concerns for their children are carried in the hearts of parents. As children's leaders and teachers, you can share those heartfelt concerns through prayer. Use the following prayer request form to let parents know you want to share in their concerns and want to pray for them and their children.

Knowing the special needs of the children you teach is vital to providing the best environment for them to learn. Parents are the best source of this information. Use the Special Concerns form to ensure the most complete and up-to-date information about each child in your class. Assure parents that information will be kept confidential.

Terrific Tips

From Our Hearts to God's Heart

✔ Include photocopies of the prayer request form with other information forms you give to parents at the beginning of the year.

✔ Keep photocopies of the form readily available for parents to pick up when they bring their children to class. You may want to have a special place for parents to return the forms.

✔ When appropriate, share prayer concerns with fellow teachers and pray together for the parent, child, or family.

✔ Set aside time each day to pray for the children in your class and their families.

Special Concerns

✔ Encourage every parent to fill out the Special Concerns form. Provide time to discuss concerns with parents.

✔ If parent concerns involve emotional traumas or significant behavior problems, you may need to seek the advice of a church staff member for the best method to meet the child's needs.

✔ Learning differences such as attention-deficit/hyperactivity disorder (ADHD) and dyslexia, as well as physical limitations such as hearing, vision, or speech problems, significantly affect classroom success. Consider different learning styles when planning crafts, games, and activities for your class.

From Our Hearts to God's Heart

How Would You Like Me to Pray for Your Child? You? Your Family?

_____

_____

_____

Special Concerns

_____
Child's Name

ALLERGIES

Environmental allergies: _____

Food allergies: _____

Craft materials my child may be allergic to: _____

PHYSICAL LIMITATIONS

Motor skill difficulties _____

_____

Hearing _____

Speech _____

Vision _____

LEARNING DIFFERENCES

Attention-Deficit/Hyperactivity Disorder (ADHD)

_____

Hyperactivity _____

Dyslexia _____

Other _____

Is your child taking any medication(s)? _____

Do you have any special concerns about your child you'd like to share? _____

_____

_____   _____
Parent's signature   Date

How Are We Doing?

"How are we doing?" is a question teachers and leaders often ask one another. But the ones who may best know the answer are the parents! Parent feedback is a great tool for evaluating the effectiveness of your teaching. Use this form to survey parents after each unit or quarter.

Terrific Tips

How Are We Doing?

✔ Have parents fill out the feedback form during a parent meeting, or ask them to take the forms home one week and return them the next.

✔ Share the results of the survey with your staff. Enjoy the affirmations your teaching brings and discuss solutions for problems parents may point out.

✔ Keep an open mind. Prayerfully consider negative comments and use them for the betterment of the class. If a parent is consistently negative, consider a parent-teacher conference or seek the advice of church staff.

How Are We Doing?

Dear Parent,

    Please let us know how we're doing! Your input is vital and valuable to us. Please respond to this survey and return this form to _____ by _____. Thanks!

Class: _____   Leader: _____

1. Please rate the following items by checking the appropriate box.

	Great	OK	Not Impressed
Lesson content	❑	❑	❑
Scripture retention	❑	❑	❑
Crafts	❑	❑	❑
Games	❑	❑	❑
Music	❑	❑	❑
Books	❑	❑	❑
Videos	❑	❑	❑
Cassette tapes	❑	❑	❑

Comments: _____

_____

2. Does your child share with you what he/she is learning in class? Yes_____No_____

Comments: _____

_____

3. What was your child's favorite Bible lesson this unit/quarter? _____

Why?_____

4. What do you like best about your child's class? _____

_____

5. What changes, if any, would you like to see? _____

_____

6. Comments or recommendations: _____

_____

5

Calling All Volunteers

Children's ministry survives only with the help of dependable, dedicated volunteers. With the forms in this chapter, you'll be able to run an organized meeting, create your own "who's who" list of volunteers, provide hints for parents, solicit and direct talents of new volunteers, and outline the volunteer qualities your program needs. You'll also find tips about how you can expand the usage of these forms into your church's other ministries.

Explore this chapter, then build up your volunteers and make your job easier in the process.

Anatomy of a Meeting

Have you ever been called away just before you were to lead a meeting, leaving the task to someone else? Have you ever been asked to step in and run a meeting at the last minute? Would you even know where to begin? Take a deep breath and read on! Just as all of the parts of your body are essential to keep YOU running smoothly, the essential components of a successful meeting are waiting for you on this form.

Terrific Tips

Anatomy of a Meeting

✔ Keep your group "on track." Use the suggested time allotments to keep your meeting moving along.

✔ Provide photocopies of this form to each person at the meeting. They'll be able to fill in the important information you discuss.

✔ Make sure you provide absent committee members with a completed copy of this form. They'll want to know what they missed.

Anatomy of a Meeting

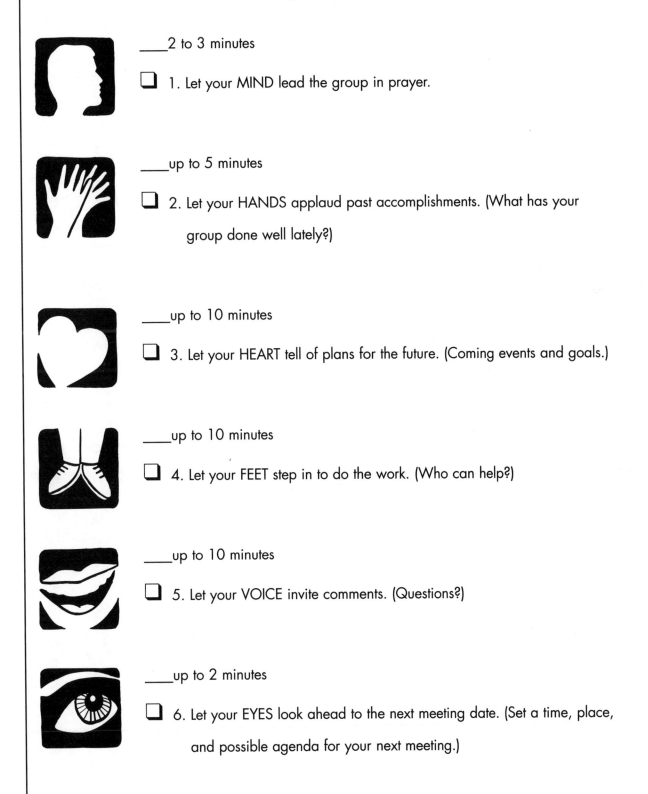

____2 to 3 minutes

❑ 1. Let your MIND lead the group in prayer.

____up to 5 minutes

❑ 2. Let your HANDS applaud past accomplishments. (What has your group done well lately?)

____up to 10 minutes

❑ 3. Let your HEART tell of plans for the future. (Coming events and goals.)

____up to 10 minutes

❑ 4. Let your FEET step in to do the work. (Who can help?)

____up to 10 minutes

❑ 5. Let your VOICE invite comments. (Questions?)

____up to 2 minutes

❑ 6. Let your EYES look ahead to the next meeting date. (Set a time, place, and possible agenda for your next meeting.)

Recruiting Volunteers

Recruiting volunteers is not always easy. Some people are not really sure of how they fit into the spiritual vision of a congregation. They can't see where they may be needed or useful. Tug at their love of children and encourage them to join your ministry by using this form.

And don't forget the teenagers in your congregation! It really hasn't been that long since they were kids themselves. Give teens the opportunity to relate to the children in their church and watch the fun—and spiritual growth—begin.

Terrific Tips

Attention Volunteers!

✔ Let this form serve as a newsletter or bulletin announcement to recruit volunteers.

✔ Use this form as a flier to further advertise your need for dedicated volunteers in children's ministry.

✔ Read the copy on this form during the announcement portion of a church service as a verbal reminder to your congregation of your need for volunteers.

Attention Youth Volunteers!

✔ Appeal to the youth in your congregation with this form before a big children's ministry event such as vacation Bible school or the annual Christmas pageant.

✔ Encourage the youth pastors to help "plug in" teen volunteers in their interest areas.

Attention Volunteers!

Dear Valued Volunteer,

On _____, _____ will begin a new and exciting
        (date)   (church name)

year in children's ministry. We are looking for dedicated Christians who are willing to make
a one-year commitment of service to the Lord's precious children.

    If you would like to be involved in the Christian development of children in our congre-
gation, and if you enjoy spending time with God's inheritance, please contact:

Name_____   Phone number_____
       (Children's Minister)

- -

ATTENTION YOUTH VOLUNTEERS!

    Do you remember a Sunday school teacher who made a difference in your life? When
was the last time you really sat down and listened to a young child? Do you need some
spark in your life? How about volunteering in children's ministry?

    We're looking for dedicated Christian youth who are willing to commit any amount of
time in service to the Lord's precious children. Contact your Children's Minister today!

WE NEED YOU!

Name_____   Phone number_____
       (Children's Minister)

Helping Hands

"What can I do?" "Where do I fit in?" "I'm not really good at anything." Maybe you've heard these comments from potential volunteers. In order to find a place for them in the ministry of the church, they need to know HOW they fit in. Everyone is good at something.

With some training, periodic feedback, and continual appreciation, children's ministry volunteers can thrive in the important jobs they are doing for children. Use the How Can I Help? and Volunteer Profile forms to help you find—and keep—new volunteers.

Terrific Tips

How Can I Help?

✔ Encourage all new members in your congregation to complete one of these forms. Let them know they have a place in your congregation's vision.

✔ Follow up completed forms quickly…don't lose a potential volunteer!

✔ Each item on the form ties directly into a ministry in your congregation. Make sure the right ministry leaders receive the completed forms.

✔ Offer a "get acquainted" training session for all new volunteers. There's comfort in knowing you aren't the only "new face" in a ministry.

Volunteer Profile

✔ Always have photocopies of this form displayed in prominent places. You never know when God will lead someone to volunteer.

✔ Make sure each new member of your congregation receives this form.

✔ Follow up immediately after receiving a completed form. Get to know your new volunteers and make them feel wanted and needed.

✔ Use the "Other" space on the form for those positions that seem to just "spring up."

How Can I Help?

Name_____   Phone_____

Address_____

City_____   State_____   Zip Code _____

How would you like to become involved in our congregation?
Check the statements that best describe you.

____ I am a leader.

____ I like financial planning.

____ I like to work in a team.

____ I like to balance a checkbook.

____ I like being organized.

____ I like to help in the community.

____ I like to be creative.

____ I enjoy going to garage sales.

____ I like working with others.

____ I like to help with fund-raisers.

____ I enjoy child care.

____ I like to teach.

____ I like Bible studies.

____ I like working alone.

____ I like listening to others.

____ I like to sing.

____ I like talking on the phone.

____ I like to play an instrument. (What instrument? _____)

____ I like the outdoors.

____ I enjoy clerical work.

____ I like to garden.

____ I enjoy drama and theater.

____ I like to write.

____ I like to fix/repair things.

____ I enjoy editing.

____ I like carpentry.

____ I am interested in volunteering but don't know where I'd be most useful.

Other expertise I can offer: _____

Please return this form to:

Name_____   Phone_____

NO-WORK PAPERWORK

Volunteer Profile

Name_____ Phone_____

Address_____

City_____ State_____ Zip code_____

Name and ages of children (if applicable) _____

Occupation_____

Areas of interest (hobbies) _____

Days you can help (Circle)   M   T   W   Th   F   Sat   Sun

Times you can help (Circle)   Morning   Afternoon   Evening

Check the positions and activities that most interest you.

____ Committee member   ____ Supplies coordinator

____ Teach Sunday school (grade level ____)   ____ Arts and crafts

____ Substitute teach   ____ Special events

____ Teacher aide   ____ Clerical help

____ Music leader/aide   ____ Furnish transportation

____ Summer Sunday school   ____ Help with fund raising

____ Vacation Bible school   ____ Service projects

____ Teacher training   ____ Parent support group

Other: _____

Please return this completed form to: _____

_____
Children's Ministry Leader

_____
Address

_____
Phone

Volunteer Code

Congratulations! You've recruited new volunteers for your children's ministry. And they have lots of questions: "What is my role?" "Who can I contact with questions?" "How long should I serve?" Use this form to organize and encourage both your rookie and seasoned volunteers.

Terrific Tips

Volunteer Code

✔ At the beginning of a church year, organize a get together where your volunteers can sign this Volunteer Code form. This will also be a great opportunity for volunteers to get to know one another before they start working together.

✔ Have all volunteers sign the Volunteer Code form on an annual basis. Each volunteer will then know his or her title, term of commitment, and duties for the coming year.

✔ Provide several phone numbers of experienced children's ministry volunteers and leaders at the bottom of the form. All volunteers will then know who to contact with questions.

Volunteer Code

Thank you for volunteering to help in our congregation's children's ministry department. We value your willing spirit, your time, and your dedication!

As a volunteer in children's ministry, you have decided to be...

Visible in your service to the Lord.

Observant, looking for ways to be of help to others.

Loving to the children you serve.

Useful in your vision for children's ministry.

Necessary and dependable.

Trained and willing to learn more about Christian education.

Excited in your service to God.

Energetic in your outreach.

Responsible to God for guidance.

In return, the congregation, children's ministry committee, and Children's Minister agree to...

Pray for you.

Listen to your needs.

Advise you of meetings, training sessions, concerns, and joys.

Nurture you in your service.

My title is _____.

My term of commitment is _____.

My duties will include _____.

FOR QUESTIONS AND CONCERNS, I CAN CONTACT:

Name: _____ Title: _____ Phone: _____

Name: _____ Title: _____ Phone: _____

Signature of Children's Minister _____

Date_____ Phone _____

Signature of Volunteer _____

Phone _____

Helpful Hints

As an adult, do you wonder how you can help a child's faith grow? As a volunteer, do you feel as though you need more insight into what a child may be thinking or feeling at church? As a children's ministry leader, do you feel that you should provide your volunteers with all the information you can find? Read on and use this form often!

Terrific Tips

Helpful Hints

✔ Give the top portion of this form to adults who have questions about a child's spiritual and emotional growth.

✔ Use the entire form for a children's ministry volunteer who may be substitute teaching or helping out with an unfamiliar age group.

✔ Send the top portion of this form home to parents during the first few weeks of a new Sunday school year.

Helpful Hints

A 2- or 3-year-old child...

- knows God loves him.
- knows Jesus is her friend.
- doesn't understand prayer but likes to participate.
- cannot sit and listen for very long.
- learns through activity and involvement.
- likes repetition.
- is VERY curious! Asks lots of "why" questions.
- has expanding language skills.

A 4- to 6-year-old child...

- wants to know that God loves him.
- wants to see how God works in her life.
- expects God to listen and answer prayers.
- understands some abstract ideas in the Bible.
- likes routine.
- is concerned about others.
- needs time to imagine and pretend.
- is beginning to reason.

A 7- to 9-year-old child...

- wants Jesus as a friend.
- wants God's guidance in her life.
- talks to God through prayer.
- is concerned about other's feelings.
- is sensitive to others' needs.
- likes cause and effect.
- enjoys a routine.
- needs time to imagine and pretend.

A 10- to 12-year-old child...

- wants to know... "Who is God? What can he do for me?"
- can have a personal relationship with God through prayer.
- is easily bored.
- is concerned about fairness.
- still needs support and guidance from parents.
- has friends who may seem more important than parents.

How I can best reach children in the following areas.

- prayer _____
- the Bible story _____
- discipline _____
- applying Christian truths to real life _____

On Call

As a children's ministry worker, do you find yourself wondering who does what in the church? Do you know how to reach the right people? Are you always searching for phone numbers when you need to call a fellow volunteer? Well, throw away your phone book and use this handy reference form when making those future calls.

Terrific Tips

On Call

✔ Give photocopies of these completed forms to each member of the children's ministry team. They'll need it!

✔ Use this form as a "guest list" for workshops, appreciation dinners, or planning meetings.

✔ When recruiting new volunteers, fill in the blanks to determine what positions still need to be filled.

On Call

POSITION	NAME	PHONE NUMBER
Children's Minister:		
Education Committee:		
Children's Music Leader:		
Sunday School Superintendent:		
Sunday School Teachers:		
Preschool—		
Kindergarten—		
First Grade—		
Second Grade—		
Third Grade—		
Fourth Grade—		
Fifth Grade—		
Middle School—		
High School—		
Adult Education—		
Sunday School Aides:		
Substitute Teachers:		
Summer Sunday School Coordinator:		
Vacation Bible School Coordinator:		
Children's Church Coordinator:		
Church Nursery Coordinator:		
Arts/Crafts Coordinator:		
Supplies Coordinator:		
Church Librarian:		
Other:		

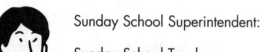

Touching Base

In business, workers need and want to know how they're doing on the job. It's the same with volunteers. What better way for volunteers and leaders to stay enthusiastic about what they're doing than to receive supportive evaluations?

If your volunteers are having doubts about their work in children's ministry, the Volunteer Evaluation form can allay fears and be a gentle guide to more productive service.

And the Volunteer Voice form can be a useful tool that provides feedback for the vision and direction of your children's ministry program. Give volunteers a voice—then make sure you listen!

Terrific Tips

Volunteer Evaluation

✔ Evaluate your volunteers at least twice a year. Touching base can help head off problems and maintain morale.

✔ Don't evaluate volunteers during busy times such as Christmas or Easter. Your results may not be typical.

✔ Complete your evaluations with prayer and a loving spirit!

Volunteer Voice

✔ Let this form be a forum for your volunteers. Keep forms handy so volunteers can share their thoughts any time they feel the need.

✔ Accept evaluations with an open mind and a loving spirit. Prayerfully consider criticism and joyfully accept suggestions.

✔ Keep tabs on your program by asking volunteers to complete evaluation forms at least twice a year.

Volunteer Evaluation

Name of Volunteer: _____

PLEASE CHOOSE A NUMBER FROM 1 TO 5 (1 = STRONGLY AGREE; 5 = STRONGLY DISAGREE) AND WRITE IT IN THE SPACE PROVIDED NEXT TO EACH QUESTION.

_____1. Volunteer seems to enjoy working in children's ministry.

_____2. Volunteer attended all training sessions.

_____3. Volunteer asked for help when it was needed.

_____4. Volunteer has completed all children's ministry responsibilities to date.

_____5. Volunteer works well with others.

_____6. Volunteer has developed a rapport with the children.

Comments: _____

_____

Evaluator: _____ Date: _____
                  (Name)

Volunteer Voice

Name: _____

PLEASE CHOOSE A NUMBER FROM 1 TO 5 (1 = STRONGLY AGREE; 5 = STRONGLY DISAGREE) AND WRITE IT IN THE SPACE PROVIDED NEXT TO EACH QUESTION.

_____1. I know what my role is in children's ministry.

_____2. I like what I am doing in children's ministry.

_____3. I have received adequate training.

_____4. I feel comfortable asking for help.

_____5. I feel support from staff and other volunteers.

_____6. I want to continue volunteering in children's ministry.

The highlight of my year in children's ministry has been: _____

_____

_____

Comments: _____

_____

PLEASE RETURN THIS FORM TO _____ by _____.
                                    (Children's Ministry Leader)   (Date)

Volunteer Screening

Unfortunately, screening the volunteers who will work with our children is a necessary procedure in today's society. Use the Volunteer Screening form as a preliminary step in choosing the best people to guide the children in your care. Be aware, however, that this form alone may not completely protect your children or your church. Check with an attorney to find out if there are other safeguarding measures you should implement.

Terrific Tips

Volunteer Screening

✔ Using this form alone may not provide complete legal protection for your church should a difficult situation arise. But it *will* show that you had the best interest of your children at heart. The more you can do to prove that you took steps to prevent potential problems, the better defense your church can present. Check with an attorney for further guidance.

✔ You may want to consider running a criminal background check on applicants. Call your local police department for information about procedures and fees.

✔ Laws vary from state to state. Some states may not require applicants to answer sensitive questions.

Volunteer Screening

Name _____

Address _____

_____

Phone (home) _____ (work) _____

How long have you been at that address? _____

Name/Address of Employer _____

_____

How long have you been employed there? _____

Are you a member of _____? _____
(name of church)

  If so, how long have you been a member? _____

  If not, what is your home church? _____

Were you a victim of abuse or molestation as a child? Yes _____ No _____

Have you ever been convicted of child abuse or a crime involving actual or attempted sexual

molestation of a minor? Yes _____ No _____

If yes, please explain: _____

_____

Do you have a current _____ driver's license? Yes _____ No _____
(state)

What do you think makes a good teacher? _____

_____

Personal References:

  Name _____   Name _____

  Address _____   Address _____

  _____   _____

  Phone _____   Phone _____

  Years known_____   Years known_____

6
Celebrate!

Want to make a kid's day? Use the forms in this chapter to make even the most ordinary day seem exceptional. Planning a party or special event? Let kids get involved with the publicity by helping with fun invitations. And don't forget the affirmations! Kids will love being recognized, and you'll love seeing them practice Christian kindness.

Alphabetic Affirmations

Kids thrive on affirmations. But how can you make sure, week after week, that you don't miss anyone? This handy alphabetic log for affirmations will help you systematically reach out to every child in your class. It will make everyone feel good from A to Z!

Terrific Tips

Alphabetic Affirmations

✔ At the beginning of the year, list all your students' names in alphabetical order. Send a note or give an award to at least one child per week or month, until you've completed the list.

✔ Keep track of students' activities in school and church. Surprise them by noticing their involvement and achievements.

✔ Take time to write a small note with every affirmation certificate or award. Kids will treasure your personal touch!

Alphabetic Affirmations

NAMES OF CHILDREN **TYPE OF AFFIRMATION** **DATE**

_____

_____

_____

_____

_____

_____

_____

_____

_____

_____

_____

_____

Awards

Awards can make the difference between feeling good and feeling GRRREAT! Hand a child an award and watch his or her self-esteem take a high jump! The following forms make affirmations easy. Use them often and watch the smiles spread. Don't wait for a special occasion or accomplishment; use these awards just for fun!

Terrific Tips

Awards

✔ Give an award to a child who needs improvement. A little encouragement goes a long way!

✔ Every month, mail an Awesome Award to a child. Make sure you mail an award to every child in your class during the course of the year.

✔ Nothing perks up a class faster than a quick affirmation. Keep photocopies of awards handy and let children fill them out for each other.

✔ Watch for kids who may be feeling down or discouraged. Then cheer them with this easy reminder of how much God loves them.

✔ If children are involved in a performance at school or church, let them know that you were watching by mailing a Pass the Praise Award to them.

✔ Recognize small acts of kindness or generosity you see in class. Maybe Jenny shared her markers with Seth or Tyler encouraged his friend who was feeling down. These are big things in little lives, and they deserve praise.

ELEPHANTS NEVER FORGET!

_____
(Date)

And _____, I'll never forget how you
(Child's name)

_____! **Great job!**
(Achievement)

_____
(Leader)

Koala Kindness Award

Presented to:

_____,
(Student's name)

On: _____,
(Date)

for kindness and cuddly character!

**"Love is patient and kind"
(1 Corinthians 13:4a).**

AWESOME AWARD

This awesome award is given to _____,
(Name of child)

on_____, for being totally awesome and wonderful!
(Date)

REMEMBER, GOD LOVES YOU!

_____
(Church)

_____
(Leader's Signature)

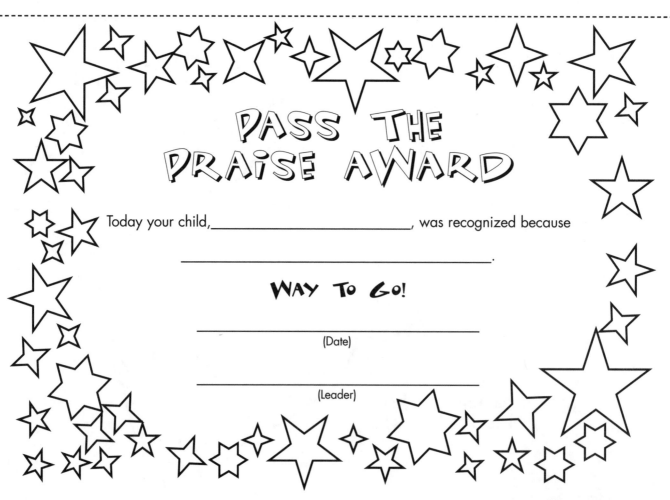

PASS THE PRAISE AWARD

Today your child,_____, was recognized because

_____.

WAY TO GO!

_____
(Date)

_____
(Leader)

Invitations

Special programs and events are great, but planning and implementing them takes a lot of time. Why not encourage your kids to help with the publicity? Let them decorate the invitations and hand them out to friends, family, and members of the congregation. They'll learn important lessons both during preparation and as they're sharing goodwill.

Terrific Tips

Invitations

✔ Make photocopies of invitations a month early and let kids help fill in the information. Incentive grows with involvement!

✔ Give photocopies of family and adult invitations to kids before a worship service and turn them loose!

✔ Keep extra photocopies available and hand them out every week for three weeks before a special event.

✔ Encourage kids to take invitations home with them and to look for opportunities to invite others to church.

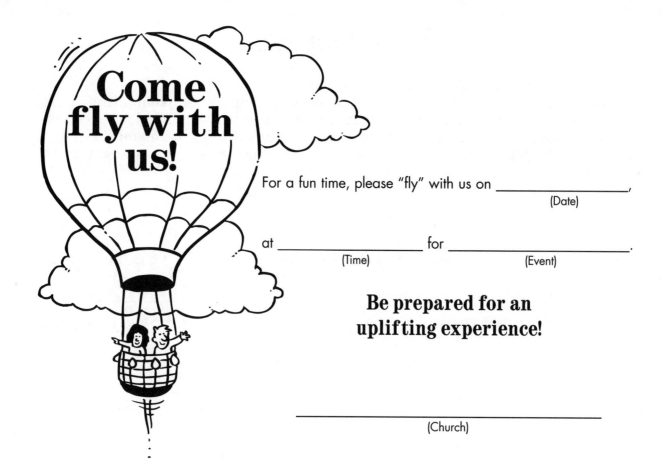

Come fly with us!

For a fun time, please "fly" with us on _____,
(Date)

at _____ for _____.
(Time)   (Event)

Be prepared for an uplifting experience!

_____
(Church)

I Want You!

I want you to come with me to

_____.
(Event)

On: _____
(Date)

Time: _____

At: _____
(Church or location)

i WANT TO HAVE LOTS OF FUN... THAT'S WHY i WANT YOU!

Many Thanks!

Nothing works wonders as much as a simple "thank you." Show your appreciation for feats great and small with this convenient form, ready at a moment's notice. Use the I've Got to Hand It to You! form to brighten a child's day as you teach the essential lesson of thankfulness.

Then use the Hats Off to You! form to thank your volunteers. Sometimes after the work is all done, everyone just moves on to the next project. Take the time to send out a quick thank you and watch the volunteers come back for more!

Terrific Tips

I've Got to Hand It to You!

✔ Don't wait for something momentous! Send a child a thank you letter for something as simple as helping to clean up the room after class.

✔ Send thank you letters after any big event that involved your kids. One way to ensure future adult volunteers is to bring kids up in a spirit of appreciation!

✔ Personalize the letter by adding a short note or drawing a simple picture with a colorful pen. Kids notice the little touches that mean you love them!

Hats Off to You!

✔ Make photocopies of this form and keep them in your office or briefcase. Then as soon as someone helps, you're ready with a thank you!

✔ Don't forget the pastor. Even shepherds need a little green pasture once in a while!

✔ Include a gift certificate for an ice cream cone with your thank you. Volunteers will enjoy your thoughtful appreciation!

I've got to hand it to you!

Thank you! Thank you,

For lending such a hand.

A friend like you is

The best in all the land!

THANKS!

_____
(signed)

Hats Off to You!

I can't keep it under my hat any longer...

THANK YOU!

**Your unselfish gifts of time and energy are sincerely appreciated.
I know your hard work in God's field will reap great harvests.**

Thanks again!

_____
(signed)

Birthday Wishes

One day a year to celebrate God's gift of life. It can seem like an empty day if no one remembers. Cards and calls can make a child's special day even more memorable. Use these birthday greetings to assure your kids that you think they're special every day of the year!

Terrific Tips

Birthday Wishes

✔ Write children's birthdays on separate index cards. Place the cards in order by dates and you'll have a handy way to remember everyone's special day!

✔ Send along some stickers with each card. Even though it won't cost a lot, kids will love the small gift.

✔ Plan ahead and let the other kids in the group sign the greeting before giving it to the birthday child.

Happy Birthday to You!

_____
(Name)

Another year to measure how much you've grown!

Happy Birthday!

from _____
(Leader)

**"But grow in the grace and knowledge
of our Lord and Savior Jesus Christ"
(2 Peter 3:18a).**

One candle, two candles,

Three candles, four;

With each passing year,

We like you more!

*Happy
Birthday!*

Love,

_____
(Leader)

Missing You

Sending a simple missing-you note is a perfect way to let someone know you care. And knowing that you care will foster better attendance and involvement in the members of your group. So if you're missing someone, don't miss out on the chance to send an encouraging message. One of the following forms can help!

Terrific Tips

Missing You

✔ Ask visitors to sign in with their names and addresses. Then add them to your master list and send them a missing-you note if they don't return the next week.

✔ Add a personal note to your missing-you message to let children know that you really remember who they are!

✔ Send cards out the day after the absence and then follow up with a phone call later in the week. Kids will love the extra attention and the chance to talk about how they're doing.

WE MISS YOU

_____, please come back!

(Name of child)

The group's not the same without "U!"

We love "U!"

_____

(Leader)

I Miss You!

_____,

(Name)

I really missed seeing you last week!

Hope to see you again soon!

I'll be looking for you!

_____

(Leader)

Get Wells and Congratulations

Life has its ups and downs, and kids need affirmation at both ends of the spectrum. When they're up, they want to share it with the world! When they're down, they don't want the world to forget them. So send get-well notes to those in your group who are sick, and watch for ways to congratulate your kids whenever possible!

Terrific Tips

Get Wells and Congratulations

✔ Kids feel as if they're missing out on everything when they're sick. So when you send a note, fill them in on what's been happening in your group.

✔ Don't wait for momentous occasions to congratulate your kids. Send them notes for the little things in life—like completing a bike race...even if they didn't win!

✔ Encourage others in your church to send notes and letters to the children. The more love a child receives, the more love he or she will have to share!

Get Well

_____,
(Name)

Hope this gives you a lift!

Get well soon! We miss you!

Love,

_____
(Leader)

*Way to Go! Hooray!
You Did It! High Fives!*

_____
(Date)

_____
(Name)

CONGRATULATIONS!

"I thank my God every time I remember you" (Philippians 1:3).

_____
(Leader)

Trips and Times Away

Studies have shown that trips and retreats can be extremely powerful tools in guiding kids toward Christ. Take full advantage of the effect these ministries can have by planning trips that teach, reach, and reward the kids in your care. Use the forms in this chapter to make your planning problem-free.

Rules of the Road

Just a few "rules of the road" can make even long trips speed by. Keep in mind that stating your expectations positively will set the tone you want to maintain. Everyone functions more comfortably when the safety net of limits is in place.

Terrific Tips

Rules of the Road

✔ Feel free to adapt or add to this conduct sheet. Kids are more likely to follow rules they helped create.

✔ Pass this list of rules out when you send home permission slips for the trip. Have both parents and children sign the Rules of the Road forms before the trip to prevent misunderstandings later.

✔ Even good rules cannot take the place of adequate adult supervision. Make sure you provide enough adult sponsors to help each child feel secure.

✔ For younger children, discuss examples of each rule to help clarify any questions.

Rules of the Road

1. Make sure to hand in a signed permission slip and release form.

2. Follow the directions of adult sponsors at all times.

3. Treat everyone with respect.

4. Stay with your group.

5. Don't distract the driver with loud talk or sudden movements.

6. If you have a problem, tell an adult.

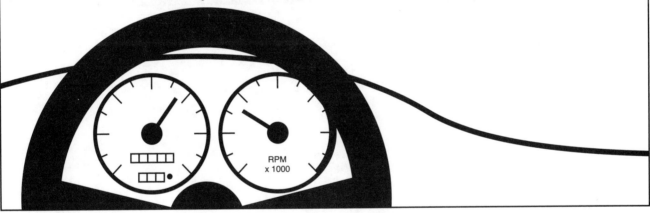

I understand these rules and will do my best to follow them. I understand that if I cannot follow these rules, I may not be able to participate in the trip.

Signed:_____
(Student)

I understand these rules and will encourage my child to follow them. I understand that if my child cannot follow these rules, he/she may not be able to participate in the trip.

Signed:_____
(Parent)

On the Road Again

Thank your drivers in advance and provide them with the best possible information for a smooth journey. This form will let each driver know who else is driving and what to expect along the way!

Terrific Tips

On the Road Again

✔ No matter where you're going, always make sure to take two vehicles. Even if one adult drives in a car alone while all the kids are in the van ahead, the spare car provides inexpensive emergency insurance.

✔ Consider renting a cellular phone for your caravan if no one in the group owns one. A phone can be an invaluable resource in any unforeseen situation.

✔ Surprise your drivers! Attach each form to an envelope containing a thank you note and quarters for the local car wash.

On the Road Again

Dear Driver,

Thanks so much for your willingness to help with this trip. We trust that it will be a fulfilling experience for our children. Thanks again!

_____
(Leader)

DESTINATION: _____

ESTIMATED DRIVING TIME: _____

ESTIMATED MILEAGE: _____

PLANNED STOPS: _____

OTHER DRIVERS: _____

KIDS RIDING IN YOUR VEHICLE: _____

_____

SAFETY CHECKLIST:

____ **GAS**

____ **BRAKES**

____ **FLARES**

____ **LIGHTS**

____ **OIL**

____ **FIRST AID KIT**

____ **PERMISSION SLIPS**

____ **TIRES**

____ **RELEASE FORMS**

Now That It's Over...

Nothing helps more in planning for the future than taking stock of the past. With this form you can quickly evaluate your trip and note any necessary adjustments while they're fresh in your mind. Use this form to note what worked and what didn't, then keep your form handy for the next planning session.

Terrific Tips

Now That It's Over...

✔ Give photocopies of this evaluation to all the adults who helped with the trip. Encourage them to return the forms promptly, and if they so desire, anonymously.

✔ Have kids give you verbal feedback, using the questions on this form to spark discussion.

✔ Express your appreciation to individuals who helped with the trip by using specific comments from the evaluations you receive.

✔ Highlight weak areas of the trip and use your findings as springboards for training sessions throughout the year.

Now That It's Over...

Please rate this trip on a scale of 1 to 5, with 5 being TOPS! Circle your answers and return to _____ by _____. Thanks!

THINKING BACK OVER THE TRIP...

Value of the Trip	1	2	3	4	5	No Opinion
Spiritual Effectiveness	1	2	3	4	5	No Opinion
Scheduling	1	2	3	4	5	No Opinion
Food	1	2	3	4	5	No Opinion
Staff Effectiveness	1	2	3	4	5	No Opinion
Kids' Behavior	1	2	3	4	5	No Opinion
Transportation	1	2	3	4	5	No Opinion
Lodging	1	2	3	4	5	No Opinion
Entertainment	1	2	3	4	5	No Opinion

THE BEST THING ABOUT THE TRIP:

SOMETHING I'D DO DIFFERENTLY:

COMMENTS FROM THE CROWD (WHAT THE KIDS SAID DURING THE TRIP):

Legal Concerns

Legal forms are a necessary part of your paperwork. A liability release form is important legal documentation to protect you and your church in case of any accident leading to illness, injury, or death. It is a precautionary document only, but one that can't be overlooked. A release form may not absolve you of legal liability. For legal questions, please consult an attorney.

Especially when traveling, nothing ensures peace of mind better than preparation. File the Transportation Release and Medical Information forms together for quick and easy reference. Make three photocopies of each: one for the church records, one for the sponsor of the trip or activity, and one for the driver in the assigned vehicle. Take care of these details before your trip, then relax and enjoy the ride.

But remember, forms alone may not provide full legal protection. For all legal questions, consult an attorney.

Terrific Tips

Liability Release

✔ No child should be allowed to participate in an outing without this signed form.

✔ Be aware that some hospitals may require a notarized release form before agreeing to provide treatment.

✔ If people have not yet returned this document 2-3 days before the trip, call to remind them.

✔ If a parent is hesitant to sign this document, encourage the parent to come along on the trip. But remember, even if the parent is present, the signed document must be on file.

Transportation Release/Medical Information

✔ These forms MUST be used in conjunction with the Liability Release form found on p. 131.

✔ Have the driver pay special attention to the allergies and special concerns of each passenger.

✔ Log in all medications, making sure you have written permission and directions from a parent for their use. Also, make sure that medication is transported in the same vehicle as the child.

✔ Do NOT give any unauthorized medication to any child. Even over-the-counter medications can cause hazardous side effects in some instances.

Liability Release

RELEASE OF ALL CLAIMS

We, the undersigned parent(s) or legal guardian(s) for _____, do hereby release,

(Student)

forever discharge and agree to hold harmless _____Church

(Church)

and the representatives thereof from any and all liability, claims, or demands for personal injury, sickness, or death, as well as property damage and expenses of any nature whatsoever which may be

incurred by my child in the course of participation in _____

(activity)

on _____.

(date)

Furthermore, we agree to assume all responsibility for any of the previously mentioned occurrences.

We give authorization for the church to provide all necessary food, transportation, and lodging (if applicable).

We give our permission for our child to participate in the aforementioned activity, and for any representative of the church to obtain necessary medical treatment. We assume responsibility for any medical bills incurred.

Should our child have to return home before the group for medical or disciplinary reasons, we hereby assume any costs incurred.

_____
Print Child's Name

_____
Father's Signature   Date

_____
Mother's Signature   Date

_____
Legal Guardian's Signature Date

_____
Insurance Company

_____
Policy Holder and Number

Both parents must sign, unless only one parent has legal custody. In such case, please indicate noncustodial parent's name and whether to contact in case of emergency.

_____
Notary   Date

_____
Physician's Name and Phone

_____
Emergency Contact and Number

_____
Noncustodial Parent/Number   Contact?

Transportation Release

We, the parent(s) of _____, do hereby give

consent for our son/daughter to ride in the designated vehicle of _____
(Church)

to go to _____, leaving at _____ and arriving at or about

_____ on _____.
(date)

Mother's signature: _____

Father's signature: _____

Signature of Legal Guardian: _____

Date: _____

Both parents must sign, unless only one parent has legal custody. In such case, please indicate non-custodial parent's name and whether to contact in case of emergency.

_____
Noncustodial Parent/Number   Contact?

Medical Information

Child's full name: _____

Address: _____ Phone: _____

School: _____ Grade: _____ Date of birth: _____

Mother's work phone: _____ Father's work phone: _____

In case of emergency and the custodial parent cannot be reached, contact:

Name: _____ Relationship: _____

Address: _____ Phone: _____

Name and phone number of physician: _____

Insurance company and policy number: _____

Any physical limitations, allergies, or medications? _____

Please note any additional details or concerns on the back of this form.

Lodging or Campsite Information Request

Nothing can take the place of actually visiting a potential overnight site, but this form will help you narrow down your choices. In addition, this form will help you be certain that you've asked the pertinent questions that will head off surprises on arrival!

Terrific Tips

Lodging Information Request

✔ Use this guide as a checklist for screening by phone and save a lot of leg-work!

✔ After screening by phone, mail a copy of this form to your top choices to obtain their answers in writing.

✔ Use the information provided by this form to reassure anxious parents that their children are in good hands!

✔ Keep these forms on file as a resource for comparison when planning future events. Update the forms annually.

Lodging Information Request

Thank you for providing us with the information we need to make lodging arrangements for our children! We appreciate the time you're taking to fill out this form.

1. What are your sleeping accommodations, and what bedding will our children need to bring?

_____

_____

2. What are your restroom facilities like, and where are they located?

_____

3. What is your locale's temperature range, day and night? _____

4. What water provisions are available? _____

_____

5. What are your kitchen services? _____

_____

Are snacks available? _____

6. Where are the nearest medical services? _____

_____

Is there 911 access in your area? _____

7. What recreational facilities are available? _____

_____

8. What is your cost per child per night, with estimated incidentals?

_____

9. Do you provide staff? _____

10. Are your facilities handicapped-accessible? _____

11. Do you provide a central meeting room? _____

12. What are your heated/air conditioned accommodations? _____

13. Are your facilities available on the following dates? _____

Get Ready...Get Set...Go!

Make sure that each child arrives with everything necessary for a great stay! Use the What to Pack checklist for the basics then add every item unique to your trip you can think of! Keep in mind any space limitations you may have, but be sure to allow room for any special "lovies" that might keep the homesick bug away!

Also, make sure parents know more than just your destination so they'll be comfortable entrusting their precious cargo to you. Give as many details as you can on the Here We Go! form. (You'll also have fewer questions to field later!)

Terrific Tips

What to Pack

✔ Sometimes noting what NOT to bring is as important as what TO bring. Make mention of these items at the bottom of the checklist.

✔ Wherever the form suggests general supplies, personalize the list to include specifics.

✔ For short trips or overnighters, you may want to limit the kids to backpacks or duffel bags that they can carry themselves.

✔ Encourage the kids to check their spending money in with you. Put each child's money in a resealable envelope then distribute the money to the children in small amounts. You may want to specify "small bills and coins only" on the checklist.

✔ Cross out any items the kids won't need for the trip.

Here We Go!

✔ Distribute this letter with all your release and permission forms.

✔ Have extras on hand to give to parents immediately before departure.

✔ Leave an extra photocopy with the church secretary or a designated contact person who will answer questions while you're gone.

What to Pack

Use this checklist to help ensure a GREAT trip!

_____ Bedding

_____ Toothbrush and toothpaste

_____ Brush and comb

_____ Extra socks

_____ Rain gear

_____ Towel(s)

_____ Change of clothes for _____ days plus _____ extras.

_____ Jacket

_____ Swimsuit

_____ Special footwear:

_____ Spending money $_____

_____ More socks

_____ Bible

Snack(s): _____

Unpaid fees: _____

Other: _____

Other: _____

WHAT NOT TO BRING:

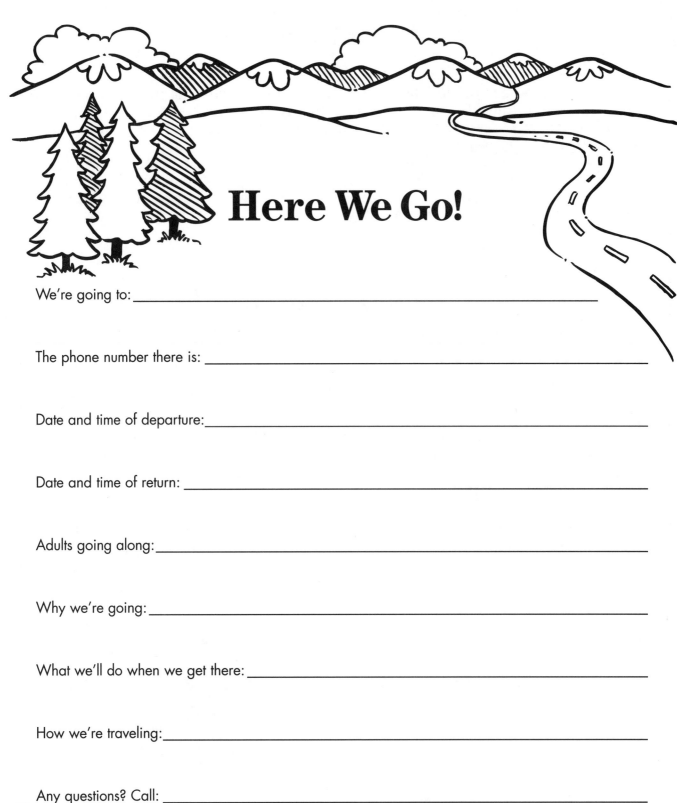

Here We Go!

We're going to: _____

The phone number there is: _____

Date and time of departure: _____

Date and time of return: _____

Adults going along: _____

Why we're going: _____

What we'll do when we get there: _____

How we're traveling: _____

Any questions? Call: _____

Makin' Plans

You'll easily check off all the important details of planning an outing with the Great Planning Checklist. Keep the form handy from the beginning to the end of your excursion. You can also use this form to file update reports with your board and follow up on your delegated tasks.

Before you shop for your trip (and after you think you've bought everything you need), check your Shopper's Checklist one last time. Think broadly and remember to plan for the unforeseen (skinned knees) as well as the inevitable (lost toothbrushes). You should be the one who "has it all"!

Terrific Tips

The Great Planning Checklist

✔ Complete this form in pencil so any changes can be easily noted.

✔ Whenever tasks are delegated, make note of the assigned person's phone number for ease in follow-through.

✔ Designate a contact person who will be available to answer questions in your absence. Make sure your contact person has photocopies of this and any other important forms.

Shopper's Checklist

✔ Even though you've tried to think of everything, make sure you plan ahead to locate the nearest store.

✔ Take inventory of all your safety supplies and equipment well in advance of each trip.

✔ In addition to a first-aid kit, gather emergency supplies that include extra toothbrushes and sample sizes of toiletries. Also, it can be helpful to have a roll of toilet paper, paper towels, and disinfectant spray handy!

The Great Planning Checklist

_____ Agenda set and distributed

_____ Publicity planned

_____ Publicity completed

_____ Reservations made

_____ Release forms distributed

_____ Release forms received

_____ Fees collected and paid

_____ Total number of children attending

_____ Children assigned to drivers and sponsors

_____ # of children per sponsor

_____ Number of drivers

_____ Purchase orders or requisitions completed

_____ Shopping completed

_____ Contact person designated

_____ Vehicles inspected

_____ ID badges made, if necessary

_____ Meeting spot determined

_____ Plan in case of rain

_____ Release forms packed

After the Fact

_____ Evaluations distributed

_____ Evaluations returned

_____ Appreciation expressed

_____ RELAX ! ! !

Name of sponsors:

_____

_____

_____

Names of drivers:

_____

_____

_____

Shopper's Checklist

GROCERIES

- On the road snacks

- Drinks

- Treats

- Food for meals

- Other

SAFETY EQUIPMENT

- First-aid kit

- Flares

- Extra blanket

- Cellular phone

- Other

SUPPLIES

- Paper products/utensils

- All-Purpose cleaner

- Pencils/Pens and paper

- Travel area maps

- Other

TOILETRIES

- Extra toothbrushes

- Shampoo

- Combs

- Other

Travel Expense Log

Keep track of reimbursable or tax deductible expenses with this easy Travel Expense Log. The sheet can be duplicated for each day of travel and for each of your drivers or sponsors.

Travel Expense Log

✔ Staple an envelope to this form to hold receipts.

✔ Carry this form on a clipboard or in a binder with any other lists you might need during travel.

✔ Turn this in for reimbursement along with a thank you note to your pastor or supervisor for the chance to participate in this ministry.

Travel Expense Log

TRANSPORTATION

Starting mileage: _____   Ending mileage: _____

$ per mile:_____   Additional auto expenses: _____

Total reimbursement: _____

FOOD

Breakfast:_____   Lunch:_____

Dinner: _____   Snacks: _____

Other:_____

Total reimbursement: _____

LODGING

Motel/Hotel/Camp accommodations: _____

Cost per night: _____

per night: _____

Total reimbursement: _____

MISCELLANEOUS EXPENSES

_____

_____

_____

Date:_____   Submitted by:_____   Approved:_____

8

VBS and Other Special Events

Vacation Bible school and other special events bring thoughts of sunshine, fun, fellowship...and hard work! Make the jobs a little easier with these timesaving forms. From awards and affirmations to friendly follow-ups, the forms in this chapter will increase your joy and minimize your work load!

VBS Theme & Development

A theme is important, but it isn't enough. Special helpers make VBS development possible. Job by job, keep track of all the important tasks your volunteers need to do. Keep your summer program running smoothly and they'll come back next year to do it all again!

Terrific Tips

VBS Theme & Development

✔ Use this form in the early planning of your VBS. Encourage committee members to brainstorm new ways to attract volunteers and new jobs for them to do!

✔ Communicate your enthusiasm! Emphasize the community outreach potential of your VBS program.

✔ Sign up willing helpers. Not everyone will feel compelled to help with VBS. But guilt will only push people away from helping on any project!

✔ Incorporate kids in your planning. Have at least one or two kids serve on the committee to decide the theme and work out solutions to problems they noticed last year.

VBS Theme & Development

VBS DATES: _____   **VBS DIRECTOR:** _____

COMMITTEES: _____

_____

_____

_____

CHAIRPERSONS AND COMMITTEE MEMBERS: _____

_____

_____

_____

_____

THEME IDEAS: (PLEASE CIRCLE YOUR FAVORITE) _____

_____

_____

LIST THE NAMES OF PEOPLE WHO MIGHT HELP WITH VBS: _____

_____

_____

_____

Match-Up

HELPER   **JOB**

_____

_____

_____

_____

Time Line

History lessons confirm the strength of a time line. It helps when remembering the past and when planning the future. Successful events have strong time lines made well in advance, then followed to a tee. Use this form any time you're planning a program, and watch as things fall into place!

Terrific Tips

Time Line

✔ Use this form in the early planning stages of any event. Let each committee member map out his or her own line, then combine the schedules into one master time line.

✔ Include on your time line any special events that will occur during your planning time. Perhaps you can use some of the events to aid in publicizing your program.

✔ Save the time line to aid next year's committee in planning the same event. VBS directors, especially, will appreciate all the help they can get!

Time Line

(Fill in dates as appropriate)

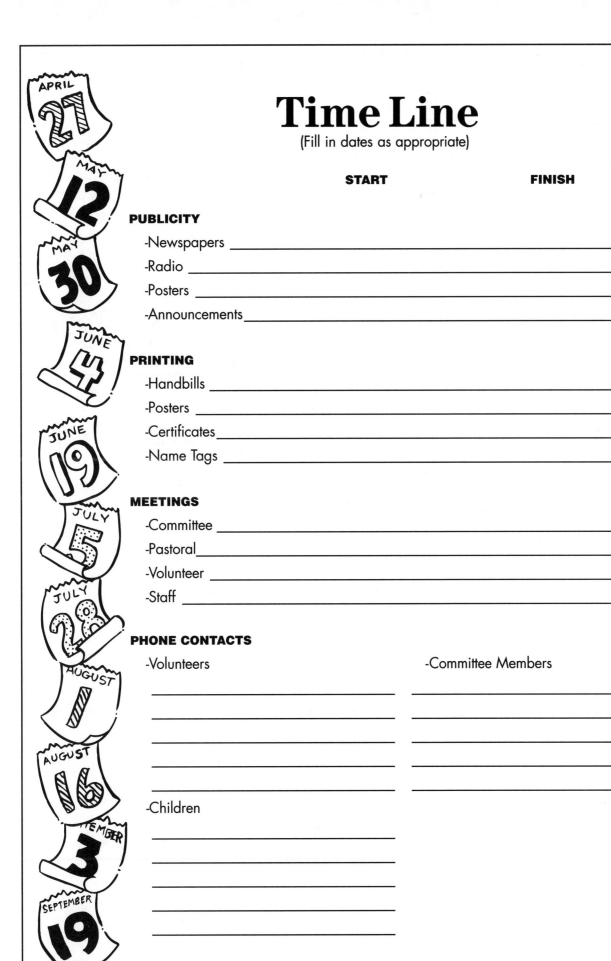

	START	FINISH

PUBLICITY

-Newspapers _____

-Radio _____

-Posters _____

-Announcements _____

PRINTING

-Handbills _____

-Posters _____

-Certificates _____

-Name Tags _____

MEETINGS

-Committee _____

-Pastoral _____

-Volunteer _____

-Staff _____

PHONE CONTACTS

-Volunteers   -Committee Members

_____   _____

_____   _____

_____   _____

_____   _____

-Children

_____

_____

_____

_____

_____

VBS Organizer

VBS generates such fun and excitement, you may have the chance to welcome new volunteers. Keep track of your workers with the handy Staff Organizer form and you'll know who's doing what during this exciting week!

Then minimize confusion and contain costs by documenting all expenses. Give each person on the committee a photocopy of the Budget Ledger and keep a close eye on expenditures. Then, when all the spending's over, look at the forms with your staff members during an evaluation meeting.

Terrific Tips

VBS Staff Organizer

✔ Use this form to help staff members envision their roles. Think of appropriate titles to go with jobs: Poster Placer, Phone Pharaoh, and Cookie Counter are all fun jobs for willing helpers!

✔ Keep this form handy during your brainstorming meetings. List possible helpers in pencil on one photocopy, then ask volunteers to confirm in ink!

✔ This form will make follow-up meetings and planning sessions for next year a snap! Ask helpers to fill out the Friendly Feedback forms on page 175. From their answers you can fine-tune the assignments for next year.

VBS Budget Ledger

✔ Attach a large envelope to this form and place it on the church bulletin board, or give a form and an envelope to each committee chairperson. Ask those responsible for purchases to place receipts in the envelope.

✔ Save the forms to aid in projecting budget needs for next year's program.

✔ To cut expenses, limit the number of people involved in purchasing. Make everyone accountable to a director or the pastor.

VBS Staff Organizer

STAFF POSITION/RESPONSIBILITY	NAME	CONFIRMED

DIRECTOR:_____

VBS Budget Ledger

ITEM	AMOUNT	INITIALS	DATE
	.		
	.		
	.		
	.		
	.		
	.		
	.		
	.		
	.		

TOTAL _____ . _____

VBS Supplies & Special Stuff

What do glue sticks, volleyballs, fuzzy cotton balls, and white paper have in common? They all could land on a list for vacation Bible school. Look over your list of games and crafts and note the supplies you don't already have on your shelves. Then use this form to make shopping easy!

VBS Supplies & Special Stuff

Terrific Tips

✔ Hand a photocopy of this list to each teacher two weeks before vacation Bible school. Then have supplies available a week ahead for double-checking.

✔ List crafts separately and compile all materials needed.

✔ Keep this form and all photocopies together for evaluation and planning meetings for next year!

VBS Supplies & Special Stuff

CLASSROOM AND CRAFT SUPPLIES

Glue or glue sticks

Construction paper

White paper

Name tags

Tempera paint

    Colors:

Pencils

Chalk

Flannel boards

Tape:

    Transparent

    Masking

Crayons

Toner

Ink

Markers

Erasers

Chenille wires

GAME SUPPLIES

Playground balls

Volleyball(s)

Baseball(s)/bats

Basketball(s)

Jump rope(s)

SPECIAL STUFF

Slide projector

Movie projector

VCR/TV

Cassette recorder

Overhead projector

Microphones

Batteries

VBS Daily Food List

All the fun at vacation Bible school makes kids hungry! Don't let keeping track of activities, games, classes, and schedules make you forget the food! Organize your snacks and kitchen helpers with this time (and mind) saving form!

Terrific Tips

VBS Daily Food List

✔ Ask an adult or youth Sunday school class to help provide snacks for Bible school. Or consider snacks the kids can make themselves.

✔ Plan your week's snacks well in advance and shop accordingly.

✔ Suggest healthy snacks such as carrot sticks, celery with peanut butter, and crackers and cheese. Cookies might be a special treat for the last day. Buy juice or soft drink mixes and prepare the beverages yourself. You'll save shopping hassles—and money!

✔ Choose an adult volunteer to direct the kitchen helpers. It's one less thing the director will have to direct!

VBS Daily Food List

Kitchen Director: _____

	SNACKS:	SUPPLIES NEEDED:	OBTAINED BY:	CONFIRMED:
MONDAY				
TUESDAY				
WEDNESDAY				
THURSDAY				
FRIDAY				

Special Program Snacks

SNACK:	PROVIDED BY:
_____	_____
_____	_____
_____	_____
_____	_____
_____	_____

VBS Daily Games

Summer games are a wonderful part of vacation Bible school. Volleyball, baseball, and relay games help kids get to know one another and enjoy themselves. Providing a variety of games throughout the week will ensure kids fun and fellowship each day! Keep track of games on this handy form and you won't forget that the preschoolers play tag on Tuesday!

VBS Daily Games

Terrific Tips

✔ Familiarize yourself with the games to be played and add any special supplies and equipment to the VBS Supplies & Special Stuff form on page 151.

✔ Encourage volunteers from your junior and senior high youth groups to help with recreation and games. Intergenerational learning works both ways!

✔ Let game time be fun. Don't try to teach every minute. Kids need time just to laugh, run, and feel comfortable at church.

✔ Keep these forms for the follow-up committee meeting. Planning for next year will be easier if you can determine which games children enjoyed most.

VBS Daily Games

	CLASS: _____	CLASS: _____	CLASS: _____	CLASS: _____
Monday				
Tuesday				
Wednesday				
Thursday				
Friday				

Teachers: Please keep track of favorite games for each class.
Let me know of any extra supplies you need!

_____
(VBS Director)

VBS Daily Music

Kids will sing the songs from vacation Bible school for years! So choose songs that will make God's love come alive in their hearts! Make sure, too, that you have all of the audio equipment you'll need for each day, ready and rarin' to go. A form like this lets you know at a glance if you're ready to make music!

Terrific Tips

VBS Daily Music

✔ Ask your VBS music director well in advance to brainstorm with you in choosing favorite songs for the schedule.

✔ Alternate program songs with just-for-fun songs your kids already know and love.

✔ Maintain a flexible heart when requests pour in. Let kids change or add to your song schedule when necessary!

✔ Check and double-check all equipment before your program begins. Make sure you have fresh batteries, tapes, etc.

VBS Daily Music

	CLASS: _____	CLASS: _____	CLASS: _____	CLASS: _____
MONDAY Songs:				
Equipment:				
TUESDAY Songs:				
Equipment:				
WEDNESDAY Songs:				
Equipment:				
THURSDAY Songs:				
Equipment:				
FRIDAY Songs:				
Equipment:				

VBS Director:_____   Music Leader: _____

Accompanist: _____   Equipment Manager: _____

Expense Log

Financial records are a necessity but can sometimes be a hassle! With a simple log for information, you can lose the last minute "budget meeting blues" and keep all your information in one handy place!

Terrific Tips

Expense Log

✔ Make a photocopy of this form for each person responsible for the purchase of materials or supplies. Help each other be accountable for maintaining good records.

✔ Maintain information in files marked for each event. Then when it's time for a budget meeting, you're ready!

✔ Attach an envelope to this form and place all sales receipts in the envelope for safe keeping.

Expense Log

Program: _____   Dates: _____

Committee: _____

Chairperson: _____

ITEM	AMOUNT	DATE	INITIAL
_____			
_____			
_____			
_____			
_____			

TOTAL _____

Posted and Announced!

A checklist is a director's safety net! Use this form to confirm that posters and announcements get from the planning stage to the bulletin board! Then rest easy knowing that people are aware of the upcoming event.

Terrific Tips

Posted and Announced!

✔ Brainstorm with others for the best placement of posters. List destinations on the form and then check them off as posters are put in place.

✔ Choose someone who will grab attention to deliver the verbal announcements. Prepare the written announcements ahead of time and allow the person to practice dynamic delivery!

✔ Keep posters and announcements simple. Fancy may impress, but it won't help people remember your event!

Posted and Announced!

Event: _____ Date(s): _____

POSTERS:

Location (Where?)	Placed By (Who?)	Posted (When?)
_____	_____	_____
_____	_____	_____
_____	_____	_____
_____	_____	_____
_____	_____	_____
_____	_____	_____
_____	_____	_____
_____	_____	_____
_____	_____	_____

ANNOUNCEMENTS:

Script: _____

_____

_____

_____

_____

_____

Announcer: _____

Dates for announcement: _____

Script: _____

_____

_____

_____

_____

_____

Announcer: _____

Dates for announcement: _____

Contact for questions: _____ Phone: _____

Come One, Come All!

Ask any kid how they feel after the first week of summer vacation and what will you hear? B-O-R-E-D! They've ridden their bikes, skateboarded, and in-line skated but have no idea what they'll do next. So share the fun with the You're Invited form inviting friends to attend vacation Bible school!

Once a child is registered in VBS, a whole new world is opened! Sunday school, church, and a firm foundation in faith may be the next steps. Use the VBS Registration Form to make sure that every child is registered, complete with phone number and address. Registration may take extra time, but eternity is worth a few extra minutes!

Terrific Tips

You're Invited!

✔ Make photocopies of this form and ask kids and grown-ups alike to add a little color to the photocopies. Use crayons or markers to give each one a personal flair.

✔ Keep plenty of extra photocopies available in the foyer or fellowship hall. Encourage kids (and adults) to take as many as they need to pass the word about VBS.

✔ Let kids know that they can use the invitations as posters to put up around town. Picture one in every window on Main Street!

✔ Let your excitement about the program show. Enthusiasm is contagious!

VBS Registration Form

✔ Ask extra volunteers to work with children filling out registration forms on the first day of Bible school.

✔ Let teachers complete forms for children who come the second day and through the remainder of the week.

✔ Use the forms for follow-up when VBS is over. Just send out photocopies of the VBS Follow-Up Letter on page 169!

You're Invited!

Are you B-O-R-E-D? Looking for some fun?
Want to make new friends? Like to play games?

Come join the fun at VBS!

_____
(Church)

We'll meet every day at:_____
(Time)

from _____ to _____
(Beginning date)   (Closing date)

If you have any questions, please call _____
(Church phone)

Can't Wait To See You There!

WELCOME! *Welcome!* **WELCOME!** *Welcome!* *Welcome!*

VBS Registration Form
Vacation Bible School

Date: _____ Church: _____

Name: _____

Address: _____

_____

Phone: _____

Age:_____ Birthday: _____

Grade in school (completed): _____

Who to contact in case of emergency:_____ Phone:_____

Allergies/Special needs: _____

_____
(signed by parent/guardian)

Welcome to Vacation Bible School!

Welcome to Our Church!

Vacation Bible school may mark the first time some attend your church. This form will help you to contact and encourage them to become regular members. How exciting to see the ministry of VBS reach not only children, but their parents as well!

Welcome to Our Church!

Terrific Tips

✔ Let kids hand out the Welcome to Our Church! forms to parents. Then have the same children retrieve the forms and deliver them to the director. Adults feel less intimidated by a child!

✔ Use the forms with care! Don't send the pastor over for a quick visit. Send a simple card acknowledging their visit to your church and encouraging them to return.

✔ Plan a VBS reunion for the week before school resumes. Use these forms to invite families for a time of food, fun, and renewed fellowship.

Welcome to Our Church!

_____
(Church)

Name of child (or children) participating in vacation Bible school: _____

_____

Parent(s) name(s): _____

Address: _____

_____

Phone: _____

Please come and join us for regular services.

Sunday church services begin at _____.

Sunday school begins at _____.

Mid-Week service is held _____.

Youth Groups meet _____.

For other information, please call _____.

We'd love to see you!

Thanks for your part in making vacation Bible school the best week of the summer!

_____
(VBS Director)

Look Who's Here!

Kids everywhere! Helpers unsure of who that little boy with Bobby is; parents unsure if they've registered or not. Keep the chaos at bay with this easy form. Keeping track of the children is an important part of Bible school and it can be a challenge! Start out with this simple form and simply fill in the blanks!

Terrific Tips

Look Who's Here!

✔ If you have a small group, set up a registration table and fill out the name and address portion of this form on the first day of Bible school.

✔ With a larger church, you may want to make photocopies of this form for your teachers and let them fill out the personal information in their classrooms.

✔ Encourage teachers to pay close attention to daily attendance. It will aid in planning next year's program.

Look Who's Here!

NAME	ADDRESS	ATTENDANCE:
		M T W TH F

_____

_____

_____

_____

_____

_____

_____

_____

_____

"And Jesus took the children in his arms, put his hands on them, and blessed them" (Mark 10:16).

VBS Follow-Up Letter

Once VBS ends, the real work begins. You've met so many new children. Who are they? Do they currently attend church? Sunday school? Send out follow-up letters to children not present in Sunday school the week after VBS. Let them know they're welcome in your church any time!

Terrific Tips

VBS Follow-Up Letter

✔ Give photocopies of this letter to each teacher on the last day of VBS. Encourage them to contact children not present on the first Sunday following VBS.

✔ If a child does not attend the final VBS program, send this follow-up letter along with an attendance certificate (page 171).

✔ Add a sticker or a picture from Bible school to personalize each letter. Kids will notice the extra care you take and it may be what draws them back to your church!

Dear_____,
(Name)

Vacation Bible school is over! What a week full of fun, music, games, and friends! Thanks for helping make it special! We would love to have you come back again for Sunday school and church.

Hope to see you soon!

_____
(Church)

Sunday school starts at:_____

Church starts at:_____

Love,

_____
(Leader)

(P.S. If you need a ride or have any questions, please call me. I would be happy to help you. We can't do the VBS week all over again, but we can get together and have fun all year! I'll be looking for you!)

Attendance Awards

Summer Bible programs are a highlight for kids. Rather than sitting at home bored, they are transported to a new world of faith-building and fun. Celebrate this special week with special awards that congratulate kids on their attendance.

But vacation Bible school is only one reason for sending an attendance award. Use this award for other special events throughout the year. Present the awards during a program or mail them in large envelopes! Kids love an award to display!

Terrific Tips

Attendance Awards

✔ Ask the teacher and pastor to sign each award personally. If possible, add a personal note to the award.

✔ Give every child an award. If they're unable to attend the presentation, mail the award with a note inviting them to Sunday school.

✔ If your group participates in service projects, keep track of kids who help out. Send a special attendance award to commend hard work and a servant's heart.

✔ Use this form for any extra activity. Kids will want to participate more when they know you care!

Amazing Attendance

This special award is given to

_____
(Name)

for attending Bible school!

_____
(Dates of VBS)

_____
(Church)

_____   _____
(Teacher)   (Pastor)

**"YOU ARE GOD'S CHILDREN WHOM HE LOVES"
(EPHESIANS 5:1A).**

Special Attendance Award

_____   _____
(Name)   (Date)

Thanks for making our event so special!

_____
(Event)

_____
(Church)

"Meet together and encourage each other" (Hebrews 10:25a).

Thanks for Your Help!

VBS without volunteers? Never! Programs without helpers? Unheard of! Hard work without a thank you? Let's hope not! Send this form as a small thank you for all the big help you've received on any program!

Terrific Tips

Thanks for Your Help!

✔ Record the names of everyone who helps with a program or event. Keep track of Joe who brought you dinner when you worked late, Mary and Laura who baked 12 dozen cookies for VBS, and each committee member who worked by your side.

✔ Write brief personal notes on the letters to tell volunteers that you remember what they contributed.

✔ Send thank you letters out within two days of the close of your program. Otherwise your thanks will be old news!

Thanks for Your Help!

Thanks for your help—you were an answer to prayer! Your hard work made more difference than you may realize.

WiTHOUT YOU, A PiECE OF THE PUZZLE WOULD HAVE BEEN MiSSiNG.

THANK YOU!!!

_____
(Leader)

"The whole body depends on Christ,
and all the parts of the body are joined and held together.
Each part does its own work
to make the whole body grow and be strong with love"
(Ephesians 4:16).

Friendly Feedback

Program evaluations can be fun! Use this form to spark some ideas and then plan a party to go over all the critiques...positive and negative! The Friendly Feedback form will help your team work together to make your next program even better!

Terrific Tips

Friendly Feedback

✔ Hand out evaluation forms the last day of VBS and ask everyone to return them Sunday morning. You can collect any remaining forms the following week. Evaluations will give you a fresh look at what everyone thought.

✔ Invite everyone to a follow-up party with lots of refreshments as a celebration! Then let them complete the forms while they enjoy the food and fellowship.

✔ Use this form to evaluate any program or event. There's always room for improvement!

Friendly Feedback

PLEASE COMPLETE THE FOLLOWING QUESTIONS IN COMPLETE HONESTY AND ANONYMITY! USE THE BACK OF THE FORM IF YOU NEED ADDITIONAL SPACE.

● How would you rate the program just completed on a scale of 1 to 10? (1 = poor; 10 = excellent) _____

● What were the program's weak points? strong points? _____
_____

● How could we minimize problems in the future? _____
_____

● Were there enough helpers to equalize the work? _____

● How could the work load be better organized or delegated? _____
_____

● Name one thing you would do differently. _____
_____

● Name one thing that impressed you. _____

● Would you like to see programs like this repeated? _____

● Last question: What is your favorite food? (When we have our next carry-in, we can provide treats that everyone likes!) _____

THANKS FOR TAKING THE TIME TO COMPLETE THIS FRIENDLY FEEDBACK FORM. IT WILL HELP US IMPROVE PROGRAMS AS WE GROW TOGETHER IN CHRIST.

Index